The Warrior Princess Submissive

MICHAEL MAKAI

the best-selling author of

Domination & Submission: The BDSM Relationship Handbook

DEDICATION

This book is for the amazing Warrior Princess Submissives in my life. May you never lose that fire in your belly, nor the sexy self-confidence that makes you beautiful to me and to the rest of the world.

Table of Contents

Preface	6
How To Read This Book	8
Introduction	12
Chapter 1: A White Knight's Epiphany	15
Chapter 2: The Other Submissives	24
Chapter 3: The Warrior Princess Submissive	32
Chapter 4: The WPS Test	45
Chapter 5: The Stealth Submissive	63
Chapter 6: Her Motivation	78
Chapter 7: Total Power Exchange	91
Chapter 8: The Switchy Feminist	102
Chapter 9: Wooing Her	113
Chapter 10: Hope And Salvation	125
Appendix A: Glossary	141
Appendix B: Silly Shit Mike Makai Says	148
Appendix C: About The Author	158

Pompey: So, why do they call you the "Warrior Princess?"
Xena: Because "Caesar" was taken.

(Xena the Warrior Princess, Episode 3.16)

Preface

Warrior Princess Submissives. I love them. *I really and truly do.*

My fascination with them is likely rooted in my twenty years of military service, some of it assigned to special operations units. I saw up-close and personal what happens to people who don't fight for what they want out of life, people who relegate the battle for justice to others. *What*, you may be tempted to ask, happens to them?

Nothing.

A whole *lot* of nothing. Nothing *good*, anyway.

I love and admire warriors of all stripes, *whether or not* they are submissives. The fact that a warrior may be a submissive, too, is just icing on the cake. And yes, Dominants like to have their cake and eat it, too. That's pretty much what being a Dominant is *all about.* We like to think we can have it all, *do it all.* There is *one* thing, however, that a *submissive* will always be able to do better than any Dominant on Earth. What is that one thing?

That one thing is *the ability to speak as a submissive, for submissives.*

You may not know it yet, but that's why you're reading this book. That's why I *wrote* this book. You and I, we're going to accomplish something *big* together, whether you really *want* to or not, whether you're a *warrior* or not. Isn't that just like a Dom? I don't even *know* you and, yet, here I am telling you what you're going to do.

I can predict the end result because, as Oliver Wendell Holmes Jr. once quipped, "A mind, once stretched by a new idea, never regains its original dimensions." You can't *unread* this book, or *unknow* what you will read on these pages. I'm *counting* on that and on the fact that you will be changed by it. If we're lucky, certain societal perceptions will also be changed over time, as well.

There is a pernicious notion held by many that being a submissive means being a *victim* or a *doormat*. The so-called *Fifty Shades* phenomenon gives this repulsive lie some very long legs, spreading it far and wide and giving it unwarranted *credibility*. This fallacy must be exposed for what it is. It is a despicable *lie* that mischaracterizes and tarnishes millions of good people living a healthy and enjoyable lifestyle. At the same time, it undermines the feminist cause, promotes *rape culture*, and ultimately *revictimizes true victims* of the very real problems of sexual abuse and violence in this country.

We're going to *fix* that, you and I.

Let's get to it, then.

Petrocles: Some people consider me
the king of sweet-talk.
Gabrielle: Well, hand over the crown, 'cause you
just met your match. When I was five, I talked my
parents into giving me my own pony.
Petrocles: When I was fifteen, I talked a
warlord into giving me his army.
Gabrielle: I once talked a Cyclops out of his
dinner. And I was the dinner.
Petrocles: I talked Xena into marrying me...
Gabrielle: You can keep your crown.

(Xena the Warrior Princess, Episode 1.14)

How to Read This Book

I am told that a preface, a "how to read this book" section, and an introduction each serve a distinctly different and necessary function. Consequently you, dear reader, are stuck today with one of each.

I typically despise the condescending practice of telling people how they should read a book, *any* book. If you're anything like *me*, you're going to read this book however you damn well please. I *get* that. I really *do*. I don't like sounding like a *book-reading-instruction-nazi*. There are, however, some compelling reasons for the advice that I am about to share with you, which I will share with you now.

When "Domination & Submission: The BDSM Relationship Handbook" - a hefty tome of *498* pages - was published, there were some readers who would reach a passage, topic, or chapter in the book that did not interest them, *and would simply stop reading the book altogether.* They apparently did not understand that *this was not a novel.* It was a lot more like a *reference book.* It didn't need to be read in any particular sequence. You really *could* just skip ahead to the next chapter without missing anything critical to your appreciation of the work as a whole. You could probably start with the *final* chapter and work your way back to the front without any problem at all.

Heck, it might even read *better* that way.

As long as we're talking about the back of the book, I would also like to point out that after the final chapter there is a glossary of terms, some random silly Michael Makai quotes, and a short author biography. For those of you who sometimes find my *verbiage* choices a little too *hoighty-toity*, the glossary can be an extremely valuable resource which really should be referred to often. For many, the glossary can be an entertaining read on its own.

There were some readers of the previous volume who had read to the last page of the final chapter and then put the book aside, without ever suspecting that there were almost fifty more pages of some pretty good stuff tucked away back there. I would advise you to just keep reading until you find yourself at the beginning of my *next* book. And no, you won't find "*verbiage*" or "*hoighty-toity*" in the glossary.

I am fully aware that many of the things I say in this book are going to be somewhat *controversial*. That's the whole *point*. I want us, as lifestylers and as a society in general, to have a healthy discussion about the BDSM culture, dominance, submission, feminism, misogyny, abuse, and exploitation.

One of the most gratifying things about having written the first book in this series was the many letters I received from readers telling me that the book helped them to understand themselves better, and was an extremely useful tool in explaining their lifestyle choices to their families and friends in a way that didn't focus solely on the *sexual* aspects of their lives. This is a national discussion that is long overdue. I *do* hope you'll help me make it happen.

Finally, a note on my practice of including personal anecdotes entitled "My Two Cents" at the end of each chapter. I began the practice in my first volume, "Domination & Submission: The BDSM Relationship Handbook," and was pleasantly surprised by the outpouring of enthusiasm for those segments of the book. A great many reviewers felt my two cents constituted the best parts of the narrative, and a few even pressed for a follow-up book consisting of nothing but such glimpses into my personal life.

I must admit that the thought of producing such a work terrifies me in ways that you cannot *possibly* imagine, since I tend to be a very private individual who does not often willingly share these bits from my past. I *do* recognize however that, without them, it would near impossible for the reader to understand the seminal experiences that have shaped my character, my subsequent D/s relationship dynamics, and my unique views on the D/s and BDSM lifestyles. Consequently, I have continued the practice of including these personal vignettes at the end of each chapter of this volume. In some cases, I've even expanded those sections significantly.

This will no doubt gratify the readers who enjoy taking a voyeuristic peek into the dusty recesses of my head and, simultaneously, infuriate the *"Just the Facts, Ma'am"* crowd. For *those* individuals - the ones who feel that personal anecdotes and opinions have no proper place in a book like this one - my heartfelt recommendation would be to simply *skip those segments.* I can *assure* you, you won't be missing anything important to the narrative.

Seriously. As far as I am concerned, the fewer people in my head, the *better*.

Prince Morlock: If I had known how much fun you Amazons would be, I'd have come to this country years ago.
Xena: I'm *not* an Amazon.
Prince Morlock: But you're so *tall!*
Xena: It's the boots.

(Xena the Warrior Princess, Episode 6.11)

Introduction

Why does the Warrior Princess Submissive merit the intense scrutiny she receives here? After all, I devoted, at best, a *page or two* to describing what I considered to be each major category of submissives in my first book, “Domination & Submission: The BDSM Relationship Handbook.” It would be entirely reasonable for my readers to wonder why the Warrior Princess Submissive deserves such special treatment in *this* book.

My *first* impulse would be to respond to that question with, “She deserves special attention because I *adore* Warrior Princess Submissives and it’s *my* book.” But that obviously wouldn’t tell the whole story and it would, in all probability, make me sound like an arrogant *ass-hat*. I may, *at times*, actually be an arrogant ass-hat, but I don’t particularly like being that *transparent*.

There are actually *plenty* of compelling reasons to take a closer look at the Warrior Princess Submissive, chief among them the fact that she is a new breed of submissive, tailor-made for the twenty-first century. She is a *stealth sub* with a distinctive paradigm, one who is motivated and sustained by an entirely different set of influences than other submissives.

The unique relationship dynamic that she shares with her Dominant is a fascinating study in Total Power Exchange (TPE) that reveals and even magnifies many of the very same mechanisms which lie beneath the surface in other types of D/s relationships yet are often overlooked by the casual observer.

She is also quite often considered to be a *switch*, at least by the classical definition of the term, which predates the contemporary application of the label to mean someone who changes his or her dominance orientation at will. The Warrior Princess is often described as a *classic* switch, which is something else entirely, and a topic we'll address fully in a chapter devoted entirely to the subject of Warrior Princess Submissive as *Switch.*

Finally, the Warrior Princess Submissive is - at least in *my* humble opinion - quite possibly destined to be the hope and salvation of the D/s lifestyle from an ever-increasing wave of attacks by a small cadre of radical feminists and misandrists who seek to equate D/s with *misogyny*.

That's right. I just called her *the hope and salvation of the D/s lifestyle.*

There isn't an iota of doubt in my mind that some of the things I've just said about the Warrior Princess Submissive will raise some eyebrows. It's entirely probable that *your* eyebrows are presently hovering perilously close to your hairline *right now*. That's entirely okay. One of the purposes of this book is to spur discussion and thought. It can't *do* that if everyone agrees perfectly with everything in it.

I'm going to do my very best to explain it all to you in the following chapters and, by the end of this book, you *might* even find yourself in agreement with some of the things I have to say.

Xena: Something about me you find interesting?
Ephiny: Yes.
Xena: Wanna tell me?
Ephiny: No.
Xena: Then stop staring at me before I take your eyes out.

(Xena the Warrior Princess, Episode 1.10)

Chapter 1: A White Knight's Epiphany

"What is she like?" my long-time close friend Jessie asked.

She'd posed the question over a large platter of nachos as we sat in a secluded booth at a trendy local steak house, celebrating her 30th birthday. Her probing question had come entirely out of the blue, totally unrelated to anything we'd discussed up to that point and, frankly, caught me just a little by surprise. Jessie, a switchy buxom amazon redhead whom I affectionately called *Red* or *Babygirl,* had an uncannily annoying habit of doing that when you least expected it.

"What is *who* like?" I asked, in return.

"You know *who.*" she replied, as she rolled her green eyes at me in her typical attitude of redheaded exasperation, "The one you've been preoccupied with for the past couple of months.

The one you drove three hours just to have lunch with. *That* who!"

"Ahh," said I, nodding noncommittally, "*Her.*"

A long, awkward silence followed, as I picked pensively at the jalapeno slices on a stack of half-eaten nachos getting soggy between us. Finally, Red simply couldn't stand it any longer.

"Come *on*, Daddy!"

Red calls me *Daddy,* and I call her *babygirl*. We have long enjoyed a deep, *platonic* love built on a foundation of D/s that defies all efforts at explanation by either of us, or anyone who knows us. I once asked her, "How long have you been a Little?" She boggled my mind when she replied nonchalantly, "Oh, *just since we first met.* Before that, I never suspected that I might be one, but something in *you* brought it out in me." For what might have been the first time in my life, I was totally speechless.

But, *I digress.*

Red continued her relentless line of interrogation. "What *is* it," she asked, "that makes her so interesting to you? I've never seen you quite so fascinated, and yet so tentative and uncertain about a woman before. I've got to admit, I *am* finding it very *entertaining*, but it's also so very unlike you, Daddy."

Now, it was *my* turn to roll my eyes. "I am *so* glad that I've been able to provide you with some measure of entertainment, even if it has to be through my own discomfort and uncertainty... *Brat!*"

She giggled in her adorably unique *babygirl* fashion and doggedly continued her inquisition without skipping a beat. "Seriously, what is she *like?* I know she *has* to be a submissive, or you probably wouldn't even be remotely interested in her. But what *kind* of submissive *is* she, and what makes her so damn special?"

I thought about it for a moment, and shrugged. "She's definitely *atypical*, that's for sure. I really don't know how else to describe her."

Red considered my answer for a moment, and then said, "Well, you described yourself as a White Knight Dominant in your book. You said that a White Knight pursues and rescues princesses. Wouldn't it be logical, then, that she would be some sort of a *princess?*"

In my previous book, I had made the case for nine major categories of Dominants. Then, finding myself at a loss as to which category I should belong, I created a *tenth* category out of whole cloth. Yes, I do know that's a pretty cocky thing to do, but that happens to be my *forte*, and they *do* say you should stick with what you're good at.

I christened this new category the White Knight Dominant, a crusading sort of Dominant who is altruistic to a fault, and who is always looking for dragons to slay and princesses to rescue. Each of the other categories of Dominants had a corresponding category of submissive in the following chapter. At the time, it had simply not occurred to me to create a corresponding category of submissive to go along with the White Knight Dom and appease the symmetry police. *Whoops.*

Interestingly enough, my omission hadn't stopped readers like Red and many others from conjuring up this mysterious, almost-mythical submissive *in their own heads* and hypothesizing upon what sort of princess might attract a White Knight Dominant *like me.* Frankly, I hadn't given it much thought at all; at least not until the question was posed to me in such a way that it forced me to apply the princess analogy to this *particular person.*

When I did, I found the comparison woefully inadequate.

Red pressed on like a pit-bull with her little interrogation. "She *is* a princess, *right?* After all, you wrote in your book that the White Knight slays dragons, and rescues princesses worthy of being Queens."

Yes, I *had* said that, and I still truly believed it. But the more I thought about it, the less like a stereotypical princess the subject of our discussion seemed. This girl was a political activist, an ardent feminist and crusader for social justice, a critical-thinking intellectual, an outspoken polyamorist, a committed and practical pansexual, a firearms enthusiast, and something of an eccentric in a whole host of other fascinating ways, as well. She was, in a word, *atypical.*

She was *clearly* not your stereotypical, *prissy* princess.

No, *not at all.*

After a great deal of thought on this subject, I finally arrived at a bit of an *epiphany*. If this woman - the object of my attention at the time - was a princess at *all*, then she was unmistakably a princess in the mold of *Xena, the Warrior Princess.*

Xena was the very charismatic and sexy character played by Lucy Lawless in the popular sword and sorcery television show which ran from 1995-2001. What most people *don't* know about the show is the fact that Xena's character was first created by the show's producers as a supporting character in another television series, *Hercules: The Legendary Journeys.*

The show's producers had originally planned on killing off Xena's character after just three appearances on *Hercules: The Legendary Journeys*, but Xena proved so incredibly popular with the show's viewers, the producers developed a whole new show around her. In the spin-off show, she was no longer a *villainess* matched against (or even *with*) Hercules; she was instead partnered with a *female* companion, a simple farm girl named Gabrielle, who not only learned to become an Amazon warrior in her own right, but did so in a way that stoked years of prurient speculation about Xena's sexual orientation!

Suddenly, it all made perfect sense to me!

This princess definitely wasn't a woman in a precarious predicament waiting helplessly for her heroic White Knight to arrive and slay a pesky dragon for her. No, *this* was a woman who, *as she is kicking the dragon's ass*, smiles over at the White Knight standing on the sidelines and says, "Hey, buddy! Feel free to jump right in and lend your sword to this fight. Otherwise, stay the hell out of my way!"

A Warrior Princess in battle is truly a fascinating and beautiful thing to see. In fact, the battleground is where she is at her best and feels comfortable in her element. For the White Knight, there will always be that temptation to simply sheath his sword and stand back to watch the subsequent carnage in awe and reverence of her indomitable fighting spirit and superior combat skills of the Warrior Princess.

As I pondered my little epiphany, I came to realize that the Warrior Princess doesn't need or want a rescuer. The Warrior Princess needs an *ally* that she can rely upon in the chaos of battle.

She seeks a warrior equal to the tasks that she has *already chosen for herself,* and she is demonstrably capable of accomplishing those tasks with, or without, his help. She is entirely willing and able to fight the good fight *alone*, but she also relishes the notion of having a worthy *partner*, fighting by her side.

When the day's fighting is done, the Warrior Princess Submissive is perfectly at ease kneeling at her Master's feet and considering herself entirely *His* - heart, might, mind, body, and soul. This is what makes her more than just a *Warrior Princess*. This is what makes her a Warrior Princess *Submissive*.

By the way, it should go without saying that anything that I *have* said or *will* say elsewhere in this book about the Warrior Princess Submissive should be interpreted to apply equally to *male* submissives with similar character traits and relationship dynamics.

In a recent D/s Radio interview I conducted with Dr. Charley Ferrer, an internationally recognized sex educator and BDSM expert, we discussed the fact that widespread gender-bias causes many people, both in and outside of the lifestyle, to assume that *any* male submissive must necessarily be powerless, weak or somehow *sissified.* She countered that fallacious argument with the example of a military general who leads armies into combat, slaying the enemy and conquering vast swaths of territory before returning home to report to and kneel before his Queen.

Is this man a powerless, *sissified* individual? No, he is *not*.

For the sake of convenience and alliteration, we will henceforth dispense with the annoyingly clunky practice of continuously acknowledging that Warrior Submissives may, in fact, be male *or* female. While that is an undeniably *true fact*, it would be highly disingenuous to claim that there is an *equal* probability of said persons being male.

A number of admittedly nonscientific studies and surveys, as well as my own personal observations over almost four decades, seem to suggest that the ratio of submissive women to submissive men who are *active* in the BDSM lifestyle is about *ten to one.* In other words, they're definitely *out there*, but not in such significant numbers that I feel compelled to torture my readers with a continuous barrage of *"he or she"* and *"his or her"* or even the grammatically masochistic and mind-numbingly improper *"they."* Yes, I do wholeheartedly support promoting *gender neutrality*, but I'm also a big supporter of writing that doesn't make blood spurt from your eye sockets. From here on out, we'll call *"him or her"* the Warrior *Princess* Submissive.

If you're going to get your panties in a bunch over it, please *get some pictures* and send them my way. I'll give you my honest appraisal.

Just one of the many services I offer.

My Two Cents: One Hell of a Woman

It might be useful for you to see for yourself what a Warrior Princess Submissive looks like in real life, up close and personal. There are so many things to love about each of the unique Warrior Princess Submissives in my life, but here are just a *few* of the things I adore about one in *particular*, whose name happens to be *Jade*.

I love the way she gives of herself from a seemingly limitless well of compassion.

She is the woman who shows up on Thanksgiving eve at the doorstep of an impoverished family bearing a box of groceries. I've watched her do this *anonymously* on more than one occasion.

She is the woman who sat in the hospital at the bedside of an elderly neighbor who was dying, a lonely old man she barely knew, because she knew he had no one to be with him at the end.

She is a woman who loves and respects even the people who don't necessarily *deserve* it. And, God knows, there are an *awful lot* of them.

I love her passion, and not just the *kinky kind.*

She doesn't just believe in something, she believes in it with a passion unlike anything you've ever seen before, and she does it so fervently that you will often find yourself *cheering her on*, even when you don't necessarily *agree* with her.

I love the way she *kicks ass* and takes names, whether it is in the professional arena, in the martial arts ring, or in academia.

As she does, she'll look over to me with a coy smile, as if to say, "They think I'm pretty *bad-ass*, don't they? But only you know the real me. *Only you.*"

She exudes a marvelous aura of empathy and *virtue*.

She is, by every definition of the term, *a good woman,* and this is self-evident to just about anyone whose path she crosses.

I love her special abilities as a muse and *synergist*. Go ahead, look it up. Don't be surprised if you see her picture right there, next to the definition. She really is *that* good at it.

In short, she is one *hell* of a woman.

"It's not easy trying to prove you're a different person."

(Xena the Warrior Princess, Episode 1.01)

Chapter 2: The Other Submissives

In Domination & Submission: The BDSM Relationship Handbook, I made the case for nine distinct categories of submissives and one additional category of what I'll call a *faux submissive*. Frankly, I will be the first to admit that these categories were somewhat arbitrarily based on historical lifestyle *traditions* in the D/s and BDSM cultures, and not everyone follows or agrees upon the same traditions and practices. I've always maintained that "right & wrong" are less valuable as tools for self-analysis and perspective on the fetish culture than the notion of *utility*. If you can find a measure of *utility* in these ideas and categories, then that makes it *right* for *you*.

For someone *else*, perhaps not so much.

There are, of course, *always* going to be submissives who are in the process of learning, maturing, and discovering themselves as submissives, as well as those who are comfortable borrowing ideas, behaviors and relationship dynamics freely from *multiple* traditions. Still others may simply be entirely *unique* or *ineffable* as submissives. There's nothing wrong with that at all.

Each person finds his or her own path. Each relationship dynamic is unique and different. *Cherish* that. Don't fret unnecessarily about why you don't seem to fit neatly into some arbitrary categorization cubbyhole.

To briefly recap, the ten general categories of submissives that I outlined in my previous work were:

The Acolyte. The Acolyte is a disciple, follower, worshipper or priestess, and considers herself a holder of sacred knowledge, a gatekeeper with the keys to her Dominant's inner sanctum, and a part of a relationship that may transcend even death in a quasi-*religious* D/s relationship dynamic. In essence, the Lesser God Dominant and his Acolytes create their own private religion.

The Brat. The brat is a submissive who is *generally* well-behaved, but has made misbehavior, teasing, and limited kinds of defiance or disobedience an integral part of the D/s dynamic she enjoys with her Dominant, preferably with his full awareness and at least his implied approval. Without the requisite awareness and approval of her Dominant, the more appropriate classification would be the *Pseudo-Sub*.

The Cow/Pig. The Cow or Pig submissive is one who enjoys being treated like a domesticated farm animal, and thrives on humiliation, degradation, and abuse from her Dominant. The relationship dynamic focuses on the real or imagined unattractiveness or worthlessness of the submissive. Cages, crates or pens are typically where the she is most comfortable.

The Domestic. Sometimes referred to as a service submissive, she is expected to perform domestic duties such as cooking, cleaning, childcare, chauffeuring, and yard work. The Domestic sub is often expected to be sexually available to the Dominant, and sometimes to his other submissives, friends, or guests. Humiliation role play is quite often a significant part of their dynamic.

The Kajira. A female Gorean slave in the tradition of John Norman's pulp science fiction novels about the planet Gor is referred to as a kajira *(plural: kajirae)*. Kajirae, almost by definition, are typically involved in relationships with Gorean Masters, however it is fairly common to find submissives who have been previously trained as kajirae but are no longer in the Gorean sub-culture and are now involved with other types of Dominants. Even so, it is quite common for certain affectations of the Gorean training to persist.

The Little. A Little is a submissive who finds joy in embracing his or her inner child. This dynamic often involves behaving, speaking, or dressing in a child-like manner or engaging in typical child-appropriate activities, and *may or may not* involve sex or other adult-appropriate themes and activities. While most Littles and their Mommy or Daddy Doms find age play to be sexually stimulating, there are also many who do not associate being a Little with sex at all.

The Novice. The Novice submissive is typically one who has very recently discovered and become excited about the D/s or BDSM lifestyle and has decided that she badly wants to be a part of it *at any cost*. Unfortunately, this often involves a frenzied and quite often very dangerous quest to find a Master - *any Master* - as soon as possible. This condition is often referred to as *sub frenzy*. The Novice submissive is easily spotted in a crowd as the sub who is lecturing anyone who will listen about her version of the *"One Twue Way"* to live the lifestyle.

The Painslut. The Painslut is usually an extreme masochist who enjoys or is aroused by sensations of intense or extreme pain. The Painslut's primary interest is pain, pure and simple, and the inclusion of the suffix *slut* is not incidental. Painsluts are often known as much for their sexual promiscuity as they are for their extreme masochism, and they tend to gravitate toward the most sadistic Dominants.

The Pet. A Pet submissive assumes the role of a cherished animal companion to her Dominant, who typically assumes the role of an owner, caretaker, trainer, breeder, or even *rider*. Pet submissives typically slip in and out of character as needed in order to deal with the more mundane and *human* aspects of their vanilla lives. The animal personas chosen by Pet submissives *generally* fall into three categories: kittens, puppies, and ponies. Many Pet Submissives will bristle at the notion that their pet personas are a manifestation of *role playing*. For many, it is an integral and *primary* personality characteristic that must be hidden from the vanilla world they have to live in. For those individuals, it is the *vanilla façade that they must maintain in public* that is the role play.

The Pseudo-sub. The pseudo-sub is someone who may be fairly new to the lifestyle and doesn't quite understand that just because she is a rope-bunny, spankophile, masochist, or bottom, that this doesn't necessarily make her a *submissive*. She typically isn't trying to deceive anyone; it's all simply the unfortunate but predictable result of erroneously assuming that just because someone is a *bottom*, she must also be a *submissive*. The Pseudo-sub likes taking orders from her Dominant, as long as he tells her to do what she would be doing anyway. A pseudo-sub is never wrong. She's just learning life lessons on her own, the hard way. The Pseudo-sub stands ever-ready to offer her Dominant advice on how to be a better partner. This usually consists of recognizing her bad moods and just *not bugging her* at those times.

We've taken the time to recap these ten categories of submissives for a couple of very good reasons. First, it is as important to know what the Warrior Princess is *not,* as it is to know what she *is*. The Warrior Princess Submissive does *not* fall under the umbrella of any of these ten submissive categories, even though there are some who might say she shares *certain* characteristics with the Acolyte and/or the Brat Submissives. I do believe that until the Warrior Princess Submissive becomes *better known* to the kink community, she will be provisionally classified as one type of *Ineffable Submissive.* Not all Ineffable subs are Warrior Princesses, but all Warrior Princesses are *ineffable*, in one way or another.

Second, revisiting the list serves as a reminder that it was this specific process of classification that served as the start of a conceptual framework for placing the Warrior Princess Submissive in a category all her own and recognizing the critical socio-political role that she is going to play in coming years. When that pivotal moment in history comes, it will seem to come suddenly out of *nowhere* and will likely be a surprise to just about everyone - *even me* - despite the fact that *I am the one who predicted it.*

Finally, it doesn't hurt to reexamine some of the basic principles and categorizations that can assist newcomers to the lifestyle, and new submissives in particular, to learn more about themselves. When they begin to ask the inevitable questions, *Who am I? What am I? Why do I feel as I do? Why do I do what I do?* perhaps you'll be able to offer some insight.

My Two Cents: The Ineffable Sub

Ineffable. *(Adjective)* 1. Incapable of being expressed or described in words. 2. Inexpressible. 3. Not to be spoken of because of its sacredness. 4. Unutterable. 5. Indefinable.

It has many connotations and meanings, to be sure. I first became aware of this rather obscure word as a college philosophy student working on a paper called *"Historical Concepts and Proofs of the Existence of God."* Again and again, in the course of my research, I found writers and philosophers referring to the purported creator of the universe as being *ineffable.* How *odd*, I would muse, to use a word to *describe* something or someone, when the word was supposed to mean *indescribable* or *indefinable*.

I forgot about that peculiar word for the next three decades, while philosophy and religion took a back seat to rather mundane priorities, like *eating* and *paying the rent*. Then, in 2013, I began writing *Domination & Submission*, and I needed a way to describe something that, at least to *me*, seemed indescribable: *Me*. Or more accurately, what sort of *Dominant* I was.

The word *ineffable* made my job just a little more *effable,* if you catch my drift. There was just one *teensy weensy little problem*. While I devoted a significant amount of ink in the book to describing the Ineffable Dominant, I somehow neglected to mention *anything at all* about any corresponding Ineffable Submissive! *Whoops*.

If I *had* to describe the Ineffable Sub, I'd say she was... *indescribably delicious!* No, wait. That's *Lucky Charms*. But *indescribable is* probably as close as we'll be able to get to classifying this submissive, who borrows freely without qualms from the characteristics and traditions of practically every other category of submissive. She may present herself as an inexplicable mixture of Acolyte and Brat - worshiping her Dominant as a God while at the same time slipping a *whoopee cushion* under his throne cushions. Perhaps she is a Novice Domestic Kajira, whose naive enthusiasm isn't dampened in the least by being chained to her vacuum cleaner. Or she could be a Painslut Pet, which might seem an odd juxtaposition for someone into puppy or kitty play. After all, who abuses or causes a puppy or kitten *pain?*

The various combinations and permutations are just too numerous to count, and just when you think you've seen or heard it *all*, someone will come along with something that *dumbfounds* you. Don't let it worry you. You shouldn't feel obligated to obtain a rational explanation for it, nor to *pooh-pooh* the notion if one is not forthcoming. It doesn't *have* to make sense to *you*.

The *only* criterion for an Ineffable Sub's eclectic *mélange* of traditions from multiple submissive categories should be this only: Does it *work* for her?

By that, I mean, is she *happy?* Is her *Dominant* happy? Does her ineffability make the relationship dynamic easier or more *difficult* for everyone involved? Is this odd mixture of seemingly incompatible submissive character traits a *natural* outgrowth of her core personality, or is it forced? Does she agonize over the fact that she doesn't seem to fit any of the traditional categories of submissive, or does she take pride in being one of a kind? Obviously, some of these questions will require *both* the Ineffable Sub *and* her Dominant to put their heads together in order to arrive at meaningful answers.

Here's the bottom line: If you *are* an Ineffable Sub, and it *does* work for you, take pride in it. Don't ever let anyone tell you that you are *wrong* for being whom and what you really are, *especially* if it makes you and your partner *happy*.

Gabrielle: Another one's fallen for you.
Xena: *Again?* What *is* it?
Gabrielle: Oh, the blue eyes...the leather. Men *love* leather.
Xena: I think it's time for a wardrobe change.
Gabrielle: Yeah. You could try wearing chainmail.
Xena: Nah. That'd just attract a kinkier group.

(Xena the Warrior Princess, Episode 2.15)

Chapter 3: The Warrior Princess Submissive

Not long after "Domination & Submission: The BDSM Relationship Handbook" was published, I began getting a large number of emails and other correspondences that all sounded a great deal like *this* one:

Dear Mr. Makai,

I have just finished your wonderful book, Domination & Submission: The BDSM Relationship Handbook and I must say I found it to be both educational and entertaining. It has opened my eyes to a great many things I had not considered about D/s relationships and the lifestyle, and it has caused me to question much of what I thought I already knew, both about BDSM and about myself.

I do, however, have one bone to pick with you, Sir. Perhaps I have missed something, but there does not seem to be a corresponding category of submissive to that of the Ineffable and/or the White Knight Dominants.

Could you perhaps explain that to me, please?

I very much regret to say that I responded to the first *few dozen* of these inquiries somewhat *flippantly*, blaming the oversight on the fact that I am hopelessly, tragically riddled with a debilitating form of A.D.D. which turns my brain to guacamole pretty much whenever I need a good excuse for making any kind of dopey mistake. It took several weeks for me to realize that these emails demanding some semblance of symmetry in my classification system *weren't* going to stop coming.

The *"mystery of the missing subbie"* wasn't going to fade softly into the night. If anything, the chorus of voices demanding an answer grew louder and louder in the ensuing months. Then, I had my epiphany about what kind of princess would be the perfect match for a White Knight Dominant, and I did the only sensible thing someone in my position *can* do when he realizes that he made a mistake. *I did the hokey-pokey and I turned myself around.*

I started writing this book. It was more than just my response to the readers who were quick to point out that there was a poor, presumably lonely missing subbie category out there somewhere. It was also a response to the large number of submissives who sent me emails, texts, and letters fretting gravely about not finding *themselves* in those aforementioned categories.

The dubiously logical conclusion that many of these readers had arrived at was that *they* must be in that missing submissive category. Some of them began to question whether they were submissives *at all.* Still others were quite confident of their own *subbiness,* yet demanded an explanation of why their type of submission seemed to have been left off my list. One adorably feisty lady came very close to challenging me to a *karate sparring match* over the issue.

Frankly, that's about when I began to seriously question the wisdom of having abandoned my A.D.D. brain-guacamole strategy.

They were *right*, of course. These readers - *these submissives* - with the *chutzpah,* the raw courage, and determination to not only *question* a supposed authority on the subject but to *demand answers* from him were *exactly* what was missing from the original list.

These submissives weren't just demanding an answer...

They ***were*** the answer.

How She is Different

As I mentioned earlier, there are some who would play the devil's advocate and argue that the Warrior Princess Submissive really isn't all that different from a Pseudo-sub Brat, or a combative Acolyte. They would be *wrong*.

Let's take a look at some of the most glaring differences that set the Warrior Princess apart from some of her sister submissives.

Her Innate Strength

The Warrior Princess Submissive not only *has* innate strength, she *exudes* it as she battles for what she feels is right and in everything else that she does. She wears her strength the same way other women wear their perfume; it is typically one of the very first things you notice about her. She is no one's doormat. *This* is definitely a woman to be reckoned with and, for lesser mortals, quite possibly even *feared*. She is intellectually, emotionally, and sometimes even physically strong and she doesn't hide this aspect of her character under a bushel. She is, at her very heart, a *fighter*. Her battle is almost always a moral crusade; she fights for *what is right*.

Conversely, where the Warrior Princess Submissive is innately *strong*, the Pseudo-sub Brat is just *headstrong* and leeches whatever power she *does* have from *others*. In the Pseudo-sub Brat's D/s relationship dynamic, as well as in other facets of her life, she is often willful, obstinate, self-centered, or reckless. This unfortunate tendency is usually one of the very first things one notices about her. She may attempt to *project* a flimsily constructed façade of strength and confidence, but that house of cards invariably crumbles *catastrophically* the moment it is tested. The Pseudo-sub Brat *considers* herself a fighter, but instead of battling *for* her Dominant, she expends most of her energy battling *with* her Dominant. The truth of the matter is, her fight is with *herself*.

The Acolyte is *also* strong, but in her own uniquely focused way. Her battle isn't so much a *moral* crusade, as it is for the

Warrior Princess Submissive, or a battle with her own inner demons, as it is for the Brat. The Acolyte's battle is an intensely *personal* one. She fights not for truth, justice, equality or any other high purpose. She fights for her Dominant, and *only* for her Dominant. Her crusade takes on a moral purpose only to the extent that her Dominant is, in her eyes, a demigod who defines righteousness and immorality *for* her.

The Warrior Princess Submissive fights for *justice*. The Acolyte fights for her demigod. The Pseudo-sub Brat fights for *herself.*

Her Self-Discipline

The Warrior Princess Submissive exercises self-discipline. It is *internal*; it springs from *within* her. She personally wields a great deal of *power*, whether that power is charismatic, vocational, political, intellectual, skill-based, or even physical in nature. She instinctively understands her responsibility to *control and channel* that power wisely because she knows that *no one else can* - not even her Dominant. Ultimately, her Dominant must rely entirely on her self-discipline and desire to please him to accomplish that goal.

Pity the poor novice Dominant who attempts to "break" or "discipline" a Warrior Princess Submissive without her explicit consent. The *best case result* in that scenario is likely to involve a great deal of frustration and humiliation for him. The worst-case outcome is a little too gruesome to contemplate.

The Acolyte depends upon her Lesser God Dominant to keep her disciplined. Her discipline is primarily external in origin. Her Dominant's approval, disapproval, rewards, and punishments are essentially all that matter to the Acolyte. She may not *enjoy* his discipline, but craves it nevertheless as the benchmark against which her devotion and fidelity are measured.

The Pseudo-sub Brat has no *self*-discipline, and is neither agreeable nor particularly responsive to any form of discipline from any external source, either. She tells a prospective partner, "You couldn't *handle* me," because she hopes that he will accept the challenge and validate her delusional belief that she is *too strong* to be disciplined. When you do, any efforts to chastise, educate, train, guide, or otherwise correct this sort of Brat submissive often result in the Dominant being labeled as cruel, insensitive, or lacking compassion. After all, it isn't the submissive's fault that she is a *brat*, and that dubious assertion eventually becomes the universal catch-all excuse for whatever misbehaviors happen to come along.

The Warrior Princess Submissive finds her discipline within herself. The Acolyte finds hers in her Dominant. The Pseudo-sub Brat has none.

Her Switchiness

One popularly held misconception about the Warrior Princess Submissive is the notion that she is a *Dominant-leaning Switch*, rather than a true submissive. The Warrior Princess Submissive often believes this about herself, in fact. This belief is based on the fact that she perceived as being *dominant* in all of her interactions involving everyone *but* her Dominant.

Indeed, this happens to be the *old-school classic* definition of a Switch: someone who is submissive to one individual or class of individuals while *simultaneously* dominant to another individual or class of individuals. That *isn't*, however, what the term has come to mean contemporaneously in the BDSM lifestyle of the 21st century. *Today*, a Switch is considered to be someone who can change his or her D/s (Dom vs. sub) or BDSM (Top vs. bottom) orientation - even in her relationship dynamic with a single individual - *at will.*

Technically, by this contemporary definition of a Switch, the Warrior Princess Submissive is *not one.* The very idea of switching her D/s orientation in her dynamic with her primary partner would seem ludicrous to her. Yet, one cannot deny that if she were to be judged by the somewhat arcane *classic* definition, she would certainly have qualified. Our inelegant but effective solution, at least for the sake of argument and analysis, will be to simply refer to the Warrior Princess Submissive as being *"switchy."* In other words, she is not *technically* a Switch, but she shares many of those same characteristics.

The Acolyte is sometimes switchy, *too*. It depends entirely upon *which* Acolyte you happen to be in the Lesser God's stable of devout disciples. Since the Lesser God Dominant cannot typically be bothered with the rather mundane tasks of managing his own flock on a day-to-day basis, he will almost always designate a high-priestess or other alpha sub to manage the others. This particular Acolyte is *switchy*, the others, not so much.

The Pseudo-sub Brat *appears* switchy at first blush, but this is primarily due to the fact that she isn't *really* much of a submissive at *all*. She often honestly *believes* that she really *is* a submissive and she even sometimes succeeds in *talking and acting* like a submissive but, at her core, she simply doesn't *get it.* You can lead a horse to water, but that doesn't necessarily make her a *duck*. Any relationship dynamic that includes a

Pseudo-sub Brat is built upon dangerously unstable ground, and will almost always disintegrate just as quickly as it popped into existence.

The Warrior Princess is switchy by being submissive to her Master, yet *simultaneously* Domme *to the rest of the world.* The Acolyte Alpha is switchy by being submissive to her demigod Dominant, Domme to her sister-disciples, and *indifferent* to the rest of the world. The Pseudo-sub Brat seems switchy in relation to *everyone* but is, in reality, often simply *conflicted and confused.*

I'd like to add a final word here about the growing contemporary usage of the term "Alpha Submissive." I've found the term to be rather perplexing, in that its meaning seems to change from person to person, morphing to fit whatever context and agenda the writers desire. Some pundits say it refers to the most alpha of a group of submissives. Others claim that it is a predominantly submissive person who switches. Still others claim that an alpha submissive is simply a submissive who doesn't really submit easily, or a brat. The term "alpha" *by definition*, means *"leader."* That would seem to preclude at least *some* of these definitions as being unworkable. My honest opinion is, the term "alpha submissive" has been, carelessly defined, inappropriately applied, and adopted by the misinformed as an umbrella term for a Pseudo-submissive.

My Two Cents: Switchy Submissives

Kristin propped herself up on one elbow as we lazed atop my unmade bed and asked, *"Master*, may I ask You a hypothetical question?"

I opened my eyes, still laying on my back, and replied with a grin, "What *sort* of hypothetical question? You mean like: If a chicken-and-a-half can lay an egg-and-a-half every two-and-a-half days, how long would it take a grasshopper with a wooden leg to sing the Star Spangled Banner backwards? *That* kind of hypothetical question?"

"No, Silly Master!" she giggled and poked me playfully in the ribs. "A *serious* question; purely hypothetical. It is not at all about how I really feel or what I am thinking... but I am *really, really* curious about what Your answer would be."

Now, it was *my* turn to be curious. *"Ask me the question,"* I said.

She hesitated for a moment, formulating her words carefully, and asked, "What would happen if someday, I were to tell You that I wanted to tie *You* up? Or if I said that I wanted to spank *You*, for a change?" I just *looked* at her, with that quirky raised eyebrow thing that I sometimes do, allowing the gesture to silently articulate my disbelief in a way that words never could.

Instant panic. Kristin's eyes widened like saucers, and her face flushed a deep, crimson red. She stammered, "No no no no *no... not me!* I didn't mean *me!* I would *never...!* I *could* never... I mean - I meant - *someone*. Someone *else!* Someone *switchy!* Seriously! Really, the thought of spanking You *literally makes me nauseous!"*

I sadistically prolonged the silent raised eyebrow treatment a few seconds longer. *"Hypothetical!!"* she squealed, helplessly.

I chuckled at her adorable discomfort and matter-of-factly said, "I would have to tell that *someone* that she needed to find a new Master."

A long, uncomfortable silence ensued, accompanied by a shocked, dumbfounded look on her face. After a time, she managed to squeak, "*Seriously*, Master? You would *release* someone because of something like that?"

"In a *heartbeat*," I replied.

She obviously couldn't believe what she was hearing. She asked, "Can you explain to me *why?"*

I said, "Because that's not the D/s dynamic I *signed up* for. It's not something that works for me, in any way, shape, or form. Just as the mere *thought* of spanking me turns *your* stomach, the mere thought of a submissive who *wants* to spank *me* turns *mine*."

Kristin thought about what I'd said for a moment, and then asked, "Well, what if someone was just playing around, being a *bratty* subbie? What if they didn't *seriously* want to spank you; they were just *teasing* or *messing* with you? *I* tease You all the time. You usually don't seem to mind!"

I nodded. "A gentle poke in the ribs or a little bit of sarcasm is *one* thing," I explained, "but any attempt to restrain me, strike me, or force me physically into a position of subjugation would *not* end well. Relationship-wise, it would be a *deal-breaker."*

To properly impress upon her the gravitas of what I was saying, I told her my *hold-up* story.

When I was in my early twenties, I attended the University of California at Riverside and worked five nights a week at an adult novelty shop in nearby San Bernardino selling porn, videos, and inflatable sex dolls. The pay was decent, the hours fit my class schedule, and business was usually slow enough that I was able to accomplish my schoolwork at the same time. As long as I didn't think too hard about the sticky floors in the back-room video booths, I had no complaints.

One night, as I always did at the end of my shift, I placed the evening's cash receipts into the floor safe that was concealed under a large flap of ratty carpeting near the cash register. I closed the safe, spun the combination dial, and replaced the carpet flap. I then stood up and turned to find the business end of a rather large pistol pointed at my forehead. Without skipping a beat, I said, *"I'll bet you want the money."*

The robber, a scraggly looking man about six feet tall and wearing a red bandana over his nose and mouth, said, "Yeah! I want the money. *Open the cash register!* Now!"

Oh wow, I thought, this moron has *no idea* what I was doing down on the floor! I nodded, which caused a minor collision between my forehead and the barrel of his gun. I opened the cash register and handed him the $50 in small bills that I'd left in the drawer. He looked at his meager haul and asked, "Is that it? *Is that all there is?"*

I answered, "Yep. It's been a *really* slow night." I shrugged.

At that point, the robber's thoughts shifted to making a clean getaway and to accomplish that, he needed to figure out what to do with me. He asked, "Does this place have a back room? Someplace where I can *lock you up?*"

"No," I lied, *"Sorry."* Another shrug.

"Fuck!" he snarled in frustration. He glanced around, desperately searching for some way to immobilize me long enough to make a clean getaway. Finally, he pointed the gun again at my forehead, and commanded, *"Lay face down on the floor!"*

I considered it for a split second, and then said, *"No."*

He was, at that point, exasperated beyond belief. *"No?? What the hell do you mean no!?"* he screamed, poking my forehead with the barrel of his gun for emphasis. "If you don't lie down on the floor *right now, motherfucker,* I *will* shoot you!"

"No," I replied, "If you're going to shoot me, you're just going to have to shoot me looking me in the eyes, while I'm standing up. I'm *not* going to lie down on the floor just so you can shoot me in the back of the head like a coward."

That was probably one of the *stupidest* things I've *ever* said or done and, believe me, I've done some *unbelievably* stupid things. I've spent over thirty years pondering all the ways it could have gone wrong but, fortunately, the bottom line is *it didn't.* The robber, apparently having exceeded his maximum recommended daily dose of exasperation, simply turned tail and ran out of the door. I called my boss, called the police, and finished closing up the shop. It really didn't hit me until the next day, how close I'd come to having a bullet put into my head.

When I finished telling Kristin the story, there was a long awkward silence, after which she sort of whistled and said, *"Geez, Master.* I knew you were *hard-headed*, but... *holy crap!"*

I nodded. *"Yep.* Unstoppable force, meet immovable object. If *that* guy couldn't even get me to *lie down*, what do you think the odds of someone *spanking me* are going to be?"

To absolutely *no one's* surprise, the subject - even as a hypothetical - never came up again.

Prince Morlock: I don't usually do this, but I'd like to know your name before I kill you.
Xena: You first.
Prince Morlock: I'm Prince Chesnick Bloodicarr Morlock, of Upper Scheherazadestan.
Xena: Xena of Amphipolis -- Warrior Princess... who conquers Prince Chesty Forlock of Whatever-stan.

(Xena the Warrior Princess, Episode 6.11)

Chapter 4: The WPS Test

Are *you* a Warrior Princess Submissive?

I should probably make one thing absolutely clear, from the very start of this chapter. The Warrior Princess Submissive is an *idealized archetypal* submissive. She is a notional prototype, unblemished and *perfect* in all of her chimerical glory.

She is Xena the Warrior Princess, Lara Croft the Tomb Raider, Red Sonja, Elektra, Wonder Woman, and Lois Lane all rolled up in one amazing stealth subbie persona. One of her most glaring faults, assuming she has any at *all*, is the sobering fact that the perfect Warrior Princess Submissive doesn't actually exist in reality. There are, however, an awful lot of people who bear an *uncanny resemblance* to her.

You just might be one of them.

The Warrior Princess Submissive Test

Let's see how closely you fit the profile, and then we'll take a more in-depth look at some of the predominant personal characteristics that make the Warrior Princess Submissive uniquely worthy of our scrutiny.

Read each of the following statements and rate your level of agreement on a scale of 1 to 5. Write the number in the space provided next to each statement.

1 = Completely disagree

2 = Somewhat disagree

3 = I don't know, or don't care.

4 = Somewhat agree

5 = Completely agree

___ **a.** I often worry that everyone around me will suddenly realize that I am not the subject matter expert at work that they think I am.

___ **b.** I often make great personal sacrifices for moral, political, or religious causes that I believe in.

___ **c.** I sometimes wonder if I am a submissive at all.

___ **d.** I find a great deal of joy in doing little things to *serve* my primary partner, like preparing a meal for him/her.

___ **e.** Most people would be extremely surprised if they know just how submissive I feel towards my primary partner.

___ **f.** Being “outed” as a lifestyle submissive would probably hurt my credibility at work or in my career.

___ **g.** Most people would say that I am a “take charge” kind of person.

___ **h.** I tend to be very opinionated about what is right and wrong.

___ **i.** I support social justice by donating money, attending rallies, or speaking out on issues that I feel deserve to be addressed.

___ **j.** I work very hard every day to make a real difference in society.

___ **k.** I would be comfortable attending a large political rally by myself.

___ **l.** My friends and family sometimes think I am not careful enough.

___ **m.** I don’t much care what people think about me.

___ **n.** I like having a romantic partner, but I don’t necessarily need one.

___ **o.** I am very good at what I do professionally.

___ **p.** I consider myself a feminist.

___ **q.** I often choose my friends based on the stands they take on moral, sociological, or political issues.

___ **r.** I often get angry or distressed when I watch or read the news and see what is going on in this country.

___ **s.** I am a supervisor, counselor, or subject matter expert where I work.

___ **t.** I often feel a lot of pressure to maintain an aura of infallibility.

Total Score: _______

Once you have recorded your level of agreement or disagreement with each of these statements, add up the numbers and compare your results with the following. Remember, this little exercise presumes that you already know, or at least strongly suspect, that you are at least a *submissive*, if not a Warrior Princess Submissive.

Compare your score to the results below. If your score is:

0 - 40: You're a lover, *not* a fighter. You avoid confrontation; you prefer to walk a path of conciliation, appeasement, and compromise. You're a *peacemaker*. You have strong beliefs and a finely honed sense of right and wrong, but believe strongly that contention and provocation is not the best way to address what is wrong with the world. Not only do you despise a fight, you aren't particularly good at it when you are forced into one.

41 - 60: You can be a warrior when *provoked.* In your own defense or when protecting your loved ones, you *kick ass and take names*. This doesn't happen all that often, however, and it makes you profoundly uncomfortable when it *does*. You may not *like* it and will typically attempt to avoid it, but you're a *competent* combatant nevertheless.

61- 80: You are *Gabrielle*, Xena's trusty sidekick. You are relatively *ambivalent* about being a warrior, but are exceptionally good in battle. You don't go *looking* for a fight, but you don't shy away from it either. Once the carnage begins, you are an excellent partner and ally in any melee.

81- 100: You are likely a Warrior Princess Submissive. You're not only an excellent combatant, you *relish* the fight; you *live* for it. Right and wrong aren't just abstract *concepts* to you; they are the foundation of what you fight for every day in your profession, politics, cosmology, family, lifestyle, and your quest for social justice. You are neither averse to, nor ambivalent about, fighting for your beliefs. In fact, you actively and consistently *seek out opportunities* to wade into the fray wherever you are and whenever you can! Fighting the good fight *makes you feel alive* and gives you purpose. It is one of the basic character traits that *define* you as a person.

Nobody's Perfect

It would be incredibly easy for someone to read some of the things I've said thus far about the Warrior Princess Submissive and think, "*Oh no!* I am *sooooo* not Wonder Woman *or* Xena! I have *weaknesses!* I am a seriously *flawed* individual. *(Insert heavy sigh here.)* I guess I am *not* so special, after all."

Wrong answer.

No one is perfect. *No one* fits the the Warrior Princess Submissive archetype *precisely.* Many of the major characteristics of the Warrior Princess Submissive will *not* apply to you. That's perfectly *okay.* Our goal here is *not* to identify you as a Warrior Princess Submissive, nor to turn you into one.

Our goal is to help you to understand those aspects of your personality - *if they happen to be present* - and to determine what, if anything, it all *means* in relation to your submission and your current or potential D/s relationship dynamic.

With this in mind, let's now take a look at some of the major characteristics that one might expect to find in a Warrior Princess Submissive.

Her Major Character Traits

She is fiercely independent.

While problem-solving, she will exhaust *all* possible options, and perhaps even some *im*possible ones, before finally asking someone for help or guidance. This woman is *so* hard-headed, you could probably crack walnuts on her noggin. One of the most difficult challenges for the Warrior Princess Submissive is to learn to *let go* of a problem so it can be handled by her Dominant or any other person. Once she masters this ability, however, she often finds it to be strangely *exhilarating and freeing*. This is one of the most fascinating paradoxes associated with being a Warrior Princess Submissive, and a major reason for her tendency towards *switchiness*.

This particular character trait is also very much related to her acute sense of competency and a tendency to suffer from *"Imposter Syndrome,"* which we'll discuss a little later in this narrative.

She is exceptionally competent.

This isn't to say that whatever she attempts to do, that she will be *uber-competent* at it. No, what it means is, she will simply go to *incredible lengths* to avoid doing anything that she *can't* excel at. Those incredible lengths will often include being *sneaky* about *why* she is avoiding certain activities or tasks. The truth of the matter is *mediocrity* is as much her sworn enemy as *evil* or *injustice*.

It is *extremely* rare to find a Warrior Princess Submissive who has settled for a waitressing, telemarketing, or any other low-wage, low-profile profession. In the rare instances that she does take such a job, she doesn't stay in it for long, because she is almost always quickly promoted to a position where she is expected to train, teach, counsel or supervise others in her *former* role. Sometimes, for a variety of reasons (some valid, others, not so much), she thinks of herself as being *too good* at what she does. Even so, that doesn't stop her from doing it uber-competently *anyway.*

She has innate strength at her core.

Her strength often manifests itself as emotional or physical toughness, determination, courage, expertise, intestinal fortitude, resourcefulness, or intelligence. Her strength is *palpable*, meaning it is self-evident to all who come into contact with her, even when she may not *herself* be aware of it. Weaker souls may be put off or intimidated by her strength, while those who are strong, themselves, instantly recognize a kindred spirit in her.

Quite often, the foundation of her inner core draws upon *subtle* forms of power and vitality such as *virtue*, *discernment*, *chi,* or *synergy*. This is why the Warrior Princess is sometimes drawn to activities like martial arts, yoga, competitive activities, and artistic endeavors.

She is a crusader.

She isn't simply *unafraid* of a good fight, she *lives* for it, and will often actively go *looking* for a fight. This is what differentiates your run-of-the-mill *fighter* from a *crusader*. The Warrior Princess Submissive is no shrinking violet. She is that dyed-in-the-wool *Republican* who attends the *Democratic* National Convention wearing a Rand Paul t-shirt. She is the African-American woman who invites herself to a *Ku Klux Klan* rally *without* a hood... and hands out business cards to everyone there. She is the woman who invites the Jehovah's Witnesses into her home and feeds them dinner, just for the opportunity to defend *Christmas* - even though she may be a *Pagan.*

When the other girls in high school or college were trying out for the pep squad or cheerleading, she set her sights on the *debate team.* While her friends agonize over how to *"fit in"* socially, she is war gaming ideas on how to change *society* to fit *her* ideals and principles. Are you someone she considers to be immoral or evil? *Run.*

She will *eviscerate* you.

Are you nodding along with this as you read it?

Tag. You're *her.*

She has a strong moral compass.

This is one of those characteristics that can sometimes leave people scratching their heads in confusion. After all, we *all* think we have a strong moral compass, don't we? Even the worst of the worst criminals will often go to great lengths to justify their bad behavior and often consider themselves to be moral creatures.

In the case of the Warrior Princess Submissive, whether *she* considers herself a moral creature is somewhat *irrelevant*. The important thing is *the rest of the world* considers her to be a person with highly-developed moral convictions, which she puts into daily practice.

This is not only relevant, but *important.*

It is important because there will come a day, in the not too distant future, when the Warrior Princess Submissive will be forced to become a combatant in a highly politicized *war* on the BDSM lifestyle. It will be a *propaganda war* that characterizes all Dominants as *abusers* and all submissives as *victims* of abusive and exploitative relationships.

When the Warrior Princess Submissive chooses to fight *for* this lifestyle instead of *against* it - as many of her contemporaries will *expect* her to do - her strong moral compass will reassure those on the sidelines that she is doing what is *right and just.*

We will discuss this very important topic at much greater length in a later chaper.

She conceals her weaknesses and self-doubt.

Her public persona is finely tuned to reveal only those aspects of her character, capabilities, environment, and inner circle she *chooses* to reveal. In some ways, she is a consummate public relations *pro* who is always massaging and filtering her *"brand"* to ensure that she is always perceived as being not only extremely *competent,* but also as being confident, capable of consistently flawless work, and completely *in charge.* This is a person who may be a *perfectionist* but, at the same time, is always painfully aware that she is *not perfect.* She is quite often an organizer who may not be terribly organized, herself. She is exceptionally intuitive and very good at analyzing and evaluating others, but not as skilled at realistically evaluating herself. She's gotten very good at *getting* answers, especially when she doesn't always *know* the answers.

She is incredibly adept at creating the impression that she *did it right the first time,* and will sometimes stay up all night long to make it *look* like a project was *simple* to accomplish. She is like the axiomatic duck, unruffled and serene on the surface of the lake, but paddling furiously beneath the surface. She makes it look easy *not* because it *is*, but because she *knows no other way*. Appearing to break a sweat, while accomplishing her miracles, is entirely *unacceptable*.

She may be *profoundly uncomfortable* revealing her flaws to the world, but she is often *absolutely mortified* at the notion of showing weakness or imperfection *to her Master.* This sometimes results in what I have come to call *sub-flight*, which is the urge or tendency of *some* submissives to withdraw or *run away* from the relationship when confronted by a sudden and intense loathing of their own very-human *imperfections*.

She is Thought to be a Dominant.

It is entirely reasonable for her friends and colleagues to assume this about her because *it's all they see.* It has always been my belief that Domination & submission (D/s) is all about *who you are.* It is a matter of where you find your joy or "happy place", and how you express your love for another in a *relationship dynamic*. BDSM, on the other hand, is *something you do*. It's an *activity*.

Situationally or temporarily *acting in a Dominant role* (i.e. in a BDSM scene, or just in the bedroom) is more accurately called *Topping*. Similarly, situationally or temporarily acting in a submissive role is called *bottoming. Acting* like a Dominant (Topping) doesn't make you a Dominant. *Acting* like a submissive (bottoming) doesn't make you a submissive, either.

To be sure, the Warrior Princess Submissive is one hell of a *Top*. She's also one hell of a *submissive.* And just in case you were wondering, *yes*, that *is* a relatively rare thing. It's *so* rare, in fact, that even the Warrior Princess Submissive *herself* often wonders how she can possibly be so good at being *both*. This smidgeon of self-doubt often results in inner conflict about whether she truly *is* a submissive, or - if so - *why*.

Sometimes, she will *erroneously* conclude that she is a *Switch*, at least by the contemporary usage and definition of the word. After all, one of the most pernicious fallacies in the BDSM lifestyle is the unfortunate notion that anyone who cannot definitively self-categorize herself as either a Dominant or a submissive *must be a Switch*.

In Domination & Submission: The BDSM Relationship Handbook, I presented a case that there were, in fact, several different categories of Switches, but that they all invariably shared one defining characteristic, which was the ability to *willfully* change their orientation. D/s Switches are able to shift between being a Dominant or a submissive, while BDSM Switches are typically able to conduct themselves as *Tops* one moment, and *bottoms* the next.

Provisional Switches comprise the category for those who simply haven't accumulated sufficient experience to be able to make a definitive assessment of their *switchiness*. The phrase *"sufficient experience"* is likely to cause a great deal of consternation or argument about what is or isn't sufficient, but it should suffice to say that anyone who has *never actually been in a D/s relationship* (regardless of how much BDSM *play* experience he or she may have) would be ill-equipped to make an accurate assessment of her own D/s or *relationship dynamic switchiness*.

Similarly, a person whose sole experience comes from a D/s relationship dynamic where the partners *never actually engaged in any BDSM activities* would probably be clueless about the extent of her BDSM *switchiness*. True, there is *typically* a great deal of overlap between D/s and BDSM, but such is not always the case.

Let's not forget that when a person switches his or her orientation, it must necessarily be *within* either the D/s or the BDSM lifestyle, rather than *from* one to the other. For example, you could switch from Dominant to submissive (or vice-versa) and you could switch between Topping and bottoming, but you couldn't switch from Dominant to bottom, or from submissive to Top.

The reason is, you don't have to. You can be *both* a Dominant and a bottom simultaneously, but you simply *cannot be a Dominant and a submissive simultaneously*. Being a Top and a bottom simultaneously is *possible*, but not terribly common. One example might be someone who engages in self-bondage, or self-spanking.

She often suffers from Imposter's Syndrome.

The Warrior Princess Submissive's inner conflict regarding her D/s and BDSM orientation often manifests itself as *Imposter Syndrome,* which is a condition which causes sufferers to believe that they are frauds who do not deserve whatever success or recognition that they have, in fact, achieved. Sufferers of Imposter Syndrome are almost always *women* who attribute their successes to simple *good luck*, great timing, the gullibility of others, or even deception on their own part. The first known references to Imposter Syndrome appeared in 1978 in the journal *Psychotherapy: Theory Research & Practice* as an article entitled *"The Imposter Phenomenon in High Achieving Women: Dynamics and Therapeutic Intervention"* by Pauline Clance and Suzanne Imes.

When the Warrior Princess Submissive suffers from Imposter Syndrome, it is typically because she is having a great deal of difficulty reconciling these two parts of her life that seem so diametrically opposed. On one hand, she is successful, powerful, competent, and universally thought of by just about everyone as a *Dominant*... yet there she is at the end of the day, kneeling at the feet of her *Master*. If all of those people could just peek into her heart and see the pure joy she feels serving Him, *they would surely realize that she was nothing but a fraud!* Of course, we know that this isn't true, but it describes *how she feels*, and it can be incredibly hard to argue with one's own feelings.

Imposter Syndrome can be an unseen saboteur of an otherwise healthy D/s relationship dynamic if it is not spotted early and addressed directly. Quite often, the mere act of recognizing it for what it is can be effective at minimizing the damage that it can do to the submissive's psyche and to the relationship dynamic itself.

Some Dominants have also found that *writing therapy*, applied in the form of *daily journaling*, can be useful in helping a submissive to sort out the D/s and BDSM aspects of her life, to see her accomplishments *in writing* and in the proper context rather than depending solely on her feelings, and allows her Dominant to provide daily *positive reinforcing feedback.*

She is *service oriented* in her primary D/s relationship

It may seem somewhat counter-intuitive that the Warrior Princess Submissive is often service oriented in her submission to her Dominant, but it is the *contrast* between what she does in her day-to-day public crusade and how she privately expresses her love and submission to her Master that provides the rationale for this dichotomy. It isn't uncommon to hear her explain it to her incredulous friends like this: "I spend all day, every day, making important decisions and telling people what to do. At the end of the day, when I want to find my *happy place*, I find a great deal of joy in performing service and doing little things for my partner, like cooking him a nice meal or laying out his clothes in the morning before he goes to work."

In spite of her *private* passion for service, she may go to great lengths to avoid being labeled as a *Service Submissive*. A service sub, which is also sometimes referred to as a *Domestic sub*, is a submissive who is expected to perform domestic duties in the Dominant's household such as cooking, cleaning, childcare, chauffeuring, and yard work. Often, she is expected to be available *sexually* not only to the Dominant, but to his other submissives and/or guests. It is also not uncommon for *humiliation role play* to be a significant part of a Service Sub's D/s relationship dynamic. Obviously, the Warrior Princess Submissive wants *no part* of anything that might *label* her in the eyes of others as a *common housewife.* Additionally, she is typically repulsed at the thought of being "loaned out" to others, and any attempt to humiliate her will likely result in catastrophic testicular loss for the person foolhardy enough to try it.

One of the natural consequences of her strong distaste for anything *"house-wifey"* or smacking of humiliation leads us to the characteristic that keeps practically everyone guessing about her, and which we will cover at greater length in the next chapter: her *stealthiness.*

My Two Cents: Imposter Syndrome

"I am *never* going to find a decent job, Master!" she sobbed, shaking her head in a fit of exasperation. Dee had been unsuccessfully searching for work for months, since leaving a good job as a university academic counselor in North Carolina to come to Texas and be with me. She had excelled and was commensurately compensated with a very good salary in her previous position but, now, that was working against her since some prospective employers considered her to be *overqualified* for the positions they had available.

I, too, shook my head, but for entirely different reasons. "Baby, what makes you say that?" I asked. "You're one of the *best* in your field. You have impeccable credentials and excellent references. You truly care about what you do and the people you help, and that is obvious to anyone who comes into contact with you. A job offer will come along soon, just wait and see. Don't give up hope."

Her tears continued to flow, as if she hadn't heard a single thing that I'd said. Her body shook uncontrollably and she cried through muffled sobs, *"No*, I'm *never* going to get hired, *because they can tell I'm a fake!"*

Her assertion seemed so completely *ludicrous* to me, I didn't quite know how to respond to it. I made a lame attempt to lighten the mood a bit. "Okay, so you're a *flake*. But, you're an *adorable* flake!" *Nothing*. No laugh, no smile... not even a momentary break in the sobbing. This was going to be a whole lot harder than I *thought*.

"All right, then, *what* makes you think you're a *fake?*" I asked her.

Her response came out in a flood of emotions, punctuated only by snuffles and tears. "They keep telling me that I'm *overqualified*, but I know what's *really* going on. They know I'm a *phony!* Somehow, they can just tell that I'm *not qualified at all!"*

I paused, in a vain attempt to digest what Dee was trying to tell me. A phony? Unqualified? Of all the words I could possibly conjure to describe her, those two words didn't come anywhere *near* being on that list. She is one of the most intelligent and capable women I've ever known, and I've known a *hell of a lot* of smart women. She has more college degrees than I have pairs of shoes. She is not just *good* at what she does, but she consistently raises the bar and *redefines the standard for excellence*. For example, when her previous employer's student data tracking system became outdated, she didn't just complain about the frustratingly substandard information technology to her superiors. *She taught herself programming for database management, and created a whole new system from scratch, in her spare time.*

Her credentials were absolutely sterling. Her professional references were impeccable. Many of them stopped just short of calling her *The Goddess of University Counseling*.

So, why was she now calling herself a *fraud* and a *phony?* I asked her, how could she *possibly* explain her perfect grades in school and her advanced college degrees? How could she have excelled in so many challenging positions, while getting raises and promotions? What about the *thousands* of students she has helped over the years? And, finally, what about *me?* Surely, I know a wicked-smart, ultra-competent, valuable outside-the-box thinker when I see one. Doesn't *my* assessment count?

“Obviously,” she sobbed, “I’ve somehow managed to *fool them all,* Master! Even you... *Even you!”* That last bit sent her right over the edge again.

I consoled her, and gently told her that she wasn’t fooling anyone but *herself.* We all knew, without a doubt, *exactly* who and what she was. She was, in a word, *amazing.* The fact that she just couldn’t *see it* didn’t make it any less *true.* She had allowed her emotions - *her feelings* - to override the *facts.*

We did some research together on the subject and found that *Imposter Syndrome* was a fairly common phenomenon which manifests itself primarily in high-achieving women. We agreed to work together to help Dee to find ways to minimize its harmful effects. Some of those solutions included letting go of perfectionism, forgiving herself when mistakes are made, acknowledging her accomplishments through daily journaling, and by relying more upon *Master’s* judgment (and not just her own) in assessing her core competencies. We also learned that simply becoming *aware* of how Imposter Syndrome can have an impact on your life can be one of the most effective ways of fighting it.

A short time later, even as the rest of the country struggled through a severe recession, Dee was offered an entry-level position at a temporary staffing agency, where she quickly earned a series of raises and an eventual promotion to management. *That* position led to an entry-level job offer at a nearby university doing exactly the kind of work she has always loved, and - *surprise, surprise* - within a year, she was put in charge of the entire department.

Kryptos: Xena?! *Two* Xena's?!
Xena: That's right. Makes you want
to cry like a baby, doesn't it?

(Xena the Warrior Princess, Episode 4.01)

Chapter 5: The Stealth Submissive

I'm guessing that until today, if you ever heard the term *"stealth sub"* at *all*, it probably conjured up images of a nuclear-powered, ICBM-carrying submarine. Frankly, until recently, it did for me, too since I just recently coined the term over a tasty cappuccino, and I did it *just for you.* I work hard, so you don't have to.

So what does it mean, this *"stealth sub"* business? It simply means that the Warrior Princess Submissive is remarkably adept at remaining below the radar when it comes to revealing herself to the world as a submissive. In fact, she is *so good at it*, she is often surprised *herself* to learn that she really is a submissive.

Let's first take a look at how she differs in her stealthiness from the other types of subs most commonly confused with the Warrior Princess Submissive.

The Warrior Princess Submissive is *stealthy* because of the very stark contrast between her dominant public persona and her submissive private one. She often bows to the prevailing winds of political correctness and public perception by promoting the notion that she is dominant in all aspects of her life. She avoids at all cost the need to explain why she is seemingly *inconsistent* to her friends, family, and colleagues. They definitely wouldn't understand anyway, and she may not entirely understand it *herself.*

In contrast, the Acolyte Submissive is *almost* as stealthy, but in a subtly different way and for entirely different reasons. She has no problem letting others know she is a submissive, but she conceals *what kind* of submissive she is. She is painfully aware of the many dangers of publicly discussing or even acknowledging the unique *private religion* she shares with her Dominant. Potential ridicule and persecution would likely come not only from the intolerant *vanilla* friends and family around her, but from many of her fellow D/s *lifestylers*, as well. Once you've been accused by your family and friends of being *brainwashed* or labeled a *whack-job*, you learn to play your cards much closer to the vest. The prime directive of an Acolyte is to shield her Lesser-God Dominant from the derision of mere mortals.

The Brat Submissive and Pseudo-sub typically aren't stealthy *at all.* Part of their rationale for being a brat (remember, the Pseudo-sub likely *thinks* she is simply a brat) is that it focuses everyone's attention on *them*. Even if they were *capable* of being stealthy, it would be somewhat antithetical to that goal.

The Warrior Princess stays under the radar *as a submissive* to avoid the dissonance between her public dominance and private submission. The Acolyte learns to be stealthy in order to protect her Lessser-God. The Brat and Pseudo-sub couldn't figure out how to stay under the radar even if it was mounted at the top of Mount Everest.

A Submissive for the 21st Century

Once we acknowledge that she *is* a stealth sub, the next logical question becomes, is the Warrior Princess Submissive a *"new breed"* of stealth submissive, or has she been with us all along? If she existed at *all* in any significant numbers during decades past, she lived surreptitiously in a world that predated women's suffrage, the growth of feminism, the LGBT movement, and the advent of a political landscape that not only *tolerates* the notion of a woman in the White House, but actually *encourages* it.

The world is just learning about her in much the same way that it reacts to the discovery of a strange new animal species that has been found in some isolated dark rainforest on a distant continent and, frankly, the world still doesn't quite know what to make of her.

The Warrior Princess Submissive may be the "stealth sub" for a new generation, but stealth subs in general are nothing new. The stereotypical 1950's *"Suzy Homemaker"* service-oriented submissives still account for a significant percentage of the submissives consciously *in* or obliviously *outside* of the BDSM lifestyle. Unfortunately, *those* stealth subs have increasingly been driven underground by the prevailing notions of the day. Surely you've recently taken note of the fact that any use of the politically incorrect term *"housewife"* is virtually guaranteed to spark a heated debate, and the term *"homemaker"* is only slightly *less* controversial.

Is it any wonder, then, that so many service-oriented or domestic submissives prefer to stay under the radar? Yet, when a Service Sub is *"outed"* the resulting contrast or cognitive dissonance between her public persona and her intimate relationship dynamic isn't anywhere near as stark and mind-boggling to outsiders as it is when a Warrior Princess Submissive is outed.

Why would this be so?

Part of the reason may be that the apparent "distance" between the stealth Service Submissive's two personas is shorter. The stealth service sub differs from the Warrior Princess Submissive in the sense that she isn't driven by the same forces (which we'll discuss at far greater length in the next chapter) nor does she project the same aura of dominance in all that she does publicly. The stealth Service Sub is typically content to appear to the world as delightfully flawed, wholly vanilla, and neither dominant nor submissive. She basically just wants the world to see her as *"normal,"* even though the word has essentially lost any semblance of meaning or relevance in recent years.

Not so, the Warrior Princess Submissive. She wants - no, she *needs* - much *more* than that. She has a compelling need to be perceived as the *best*, the *smartest*, the *strongest*, or the *most capable* at what she does. She thinks: Why be normal, or even try to appear as such? *Normality is for the mediocre.*

A warrior doesn't seek to blend in with the crowd. A warrior steps out in front and rallies the troops or becomes the standard-bearer. This is what makes the Warrior Princess Submissive, at least in her *public persona*, a *crusader*. It is also what makes her seem, to the rest of the world, to be a *Dominant*.

This wide gulf between her crusading and dominant public persona and the intimate submissive relationship dynamic that she enjoys with her partner often mystifies and troubles the Warrior Princess Submissive when she takes the time for some quiet self-reflection. She sometimes worries that her natural and comforting sense of submission to her partner will be perceived by others as *weakness* or as a *character flaw*.

She also sometimes has a great deal of difficulty reconciling her *innate and heartfelt feminism* (which we will explore further in a subsequent chapter) with her deep desire to express her love for her partner through submission. There is, in fact, no inherent contradiction or incompatibility between her submission and her feminism, but she may not *know* that... *yet*.

My Two Cents: Stealth vs. Deceit

A Warrior Princess Submissive may be *stealthy*, but that doesn't necessarily make her *deceitful*. It just makes her *smart*. On the other hand, there are some submissives who are *not* Warrior Princesses, *not* stealthy, and *not* smart. Some are just plain *deceitful*. This is the story of one such sub.

Fair warning: This story does *not* have a happy ending. In fact, I would go so far as to characterize it as a catastrophically *bad* ending. If you'd like to just skip ahead *now* to the next chapter, I won't think any less of you, *I promise.*

I am also painfully aware of the fact that the story is overly *long*, but I am unwilling to shorten it simply for the sake of brevity. The fact that this story describes relatively recent events in my admittedly peculiar life makes it all the more difficult and painful to tell. Even so, I made a pact with myself at the beginning of this project to share these tales with you in the hopes that you may be able to dodge some of the train wrecks that I have *failed* to avoid.

Her name was *Valerie*. I became acquainted with her while moderating an online BDSM chat room at about the same time that I was putting the finishing touches on the manuscript for my first book. She was an attractive 25-year old single mother of two young boys in Biloxi, Mississippi. My initial appraisal of her was that she was extremely head-strong, intelligent, creative, and refreshingly outspoken. This charming and flirtatious southern belle told me she was *very* curious about both the BDSM and poly lifestyles, and asked me if I would teach her. After giving it some thought, I told her that I would.

Over the course of the next several weeks, we got to know each other better and developed a close long-distance relationship, as oxymoronic as that may sound. Eventually, we transitioned from online text chats to frequent telephone and Skype voice calls, and even began discussing whether we should meet in real life.

At about the same time, I began formulating my thoughts and jotting notes on the Warrior Princess Submissive in preparation for this book. When I described the Warrior Princess Submissive to her, she perked and grew very excited, exclaiming, "*Oh my god, that's me!* That describes me *perfectly!*" She went on to say that, even though she considered herself to be a true submissive, no one *else* would ever characterize her that way. She also described in vivid detail what a *survivor, fighter, and crusader* she considered herself to be. She told me about how she had survived being sexually abused by *several* of her family members as a child, being physically beaten by her father to the point of being hospitalized *seven times*, and of surviving an actual *murder attempt* by her ex-husband. She also told me that, as a result of that childhood sexual abuse, the beatings, and of *being locked in a car and set on fire by her ex-husband,* she had been diagnosed with post-traumatic stress syndrome (PTSD) and bi-polar disorder, and was placed on full disability, which was her sole source of income.

In retrospect, that *should* have been my first major clue that Valerie was nowhere *near* ready to tackle *any* sort of committed relationship of *any* kind, much *less* a D/s relationship chock-full of *BDSM and polyamory*. Did I *listen* to the warning bells that were sounding in the back of my head?

No, *I did not.*

I did not really believe at the time that Valerie was a Warrior Princess Submissive, but I didn't see the harm in allowing her to *think* she was, since her self-esteem seemed to need a great deal of bolstering at the time. Besides, I was still formulating my thoughts on the subject and hadn't as yet arrived at any firm criteria. To further complicate matters, my *"White Knight Syndrome"* had seriously begun to undermine my rationality. I just wanted to *help* this poor woman in any way that I could. In my *own* mind, that meant teaching her, advising her, guiding her, mentoring her. In *her* mind, the optimal solution would be for me to ride in on a white stallion to whisk her and her boys away to Texas to be with me, and she said as much on many occasions. My response was always that such talk was *way* too premature, and shouldn't even be considered until we had at *least* met in real life. She would always respond in turn with, "Well then, *let's meet!"* and would attempt to convince me further by sending me flirty, semi-nude photos of herself. Frankly, my already compromised rationality was pretty *gone* by that point.

Whenever she said we should meet, I would almost always say something like, "Be careful what you *wish* for," or "*Anything* is possible!" It sometimes takes people a while to realize that I may be laughing when I *say* such things, but I am almost always *serious*. On more than one occasion, I had calculated the driving time and cost of gasoline for a trip to Biloxi and back, just in case I got bored one weekend.

One night, as we chatted about the events of our day, Valerie mentioned that she was *terrified* because a woman she knew casually had just been *murdered* and her corpse left in the woods adjacent to the trailer park where she lived. Since I happen to be an information addict, I immediately began scanning the internet for more information about the murder.

Over the course of the next few days, I found absolutely *nothing*. I kept asking myself, how many trailer parks and/or ongoing murder investigations can there *be* in a city the size of Biloxi, and why isn't there any information on either? The answer, of course, was that there was no information on it because it *never happened*; at least, *not in Biloxi, Mississippi.*

After a few days, I confronted her with my suspicions, and she confessed. She wasn't in Biloxi *at all.* That had been a simple ruse to protect her from the many creeps and jerks one regularly encounters in internet chat rooms. She told me that her *actual* location was a small town in *Virginia*. She apologized profusely for the deception and begged for my forgiveness, which I gave. Even so, the alarm bells in my head were sounding much louder now, and I resolved to find out soon what *else* she may have lied about.

A few days later, I called her at about 8 o'clock in the morning and asked, "What are you going to be doing today, around lunchtime?"

She replied somewhat hesitantly, "Nothing, *why?*"

I said, "I'm on my way to the airport right now. I should be in Virginia by *lunchtime*. I thought maybe we could perhaps meet for a cup of coffee..."

Click.

She'd *hung up on me!* She didn't even let me get to the part about my reason for flying to the east coast, which was *to see my sister,* who happens to live in the Washington D.C. area. I tried calling her back. No answer. When I arrived at the airport, I tried again. This time, I got a recording: *"The number you are calling is no longer in service."* Curiouser and curiouser.

As I waited on my flight, I began checking some of the other ways we regularly communicated, and found that I'd been *unfriended and blocked* on Skype, Facebook, and a few other chat programs. Her email address suddenly no longer existed. This woman *seriously* didn't want to be found, and *that* only served to stoke my curiosity even *more*. I had thirty minutes to kill before boarding my flight, so I used that time to do a little internet sleuthing. By the time my flight was called, I'd tracked her IP to a specific address. *No*, I wasn't going to *confront* her. *That* would be seriously *creepy*. But I *was* going to satisfy my curiosity to the greatest extent possible, without breaking any laws or spending the night in a small-town Virginia jail cell.

I got off the plane, rented a car, and drove to the address to which I'd tracked her. The trailer park was, frankly, a *dump*. It didn't take much imagination at *all* to see why someone had dumped a corpse in the nearby woods. A slow drive through the complex helped me to identify her trailer, which was pretty much as she'd described it to me in our many talks. *Something* didn't seem right, though. I finally realized what it was. Not only was the trailer way too *small* for a mother and her two school-aged boys, but there were none of the things one might expect to find in the yard if there *were* really two rambunctious youngsters living there. No toys. No bikes or scooters. Nothing *fun* at *all*. I made a few mental notations about what I observed, and then left to visit my sister and some other friends a few hours north.

About a week later, I received a text message from an unknown number. It said, "This is Valerie. I need to video Skype with you. *Please*." I pulled out my laptop and fired up my Skype, and took our first video call. There, on my screen, was someone I'd never seen before. Her *voice* was the same, but the *face* didn't match the many photos that she'd sent to me over the last few months, and she was *clearly* not 25 years old. She was sobbing. Her face was swollen and red. Her hair was a mess.

"I am so, so sorry, Sir." she sobbed. *"This* is the *real* me. I'm *not* 25 years old, I'm 47 years old. The pictures I sent to you were pictures of my *daughter*, not me. *She's* the one with the two boys, *not me*. They're my *grandkids*. I told you I was divorced, and I *am*, but *she* is happily married. Her husband doesn't know I sent you sexy pictures of her, or made you think he was an ass. She gave me the pictures because I told her I wanted to play a joke on someone. Everything *else* that I told you was *true*. I'm still the *same person.*

"No, Valerie," I said, "You're *not.* Not even *close*. What did you hope to accomplish? *Where in the world* did you think this was all going to end up?"

"I... I... don't know!" she cried. "When I first met you online, I thought you were just another *phony Dom.* I figured I would mess with your head a little, maybe seduce you, and then expose you as a jerk and a phony Dom. I figured it would be a lot easier if I pretended to be my daughter. But then I found out that you were the *real thing*. And then, *I fell in love with you.* By then, it was *too late* to tell you the truth. I was stuck with the lie."

I nodded. "So, when you thought I was coming specifically to see you, you panicked."

"Yes, Sir." she whimpered, with downcast eyes. "I didn't want you to see that I was *old.* And *fat*. And a *drunk*, and a *liar*." With that, her whimpering turned into *wailing*. *"Please, Sir! Please* give me another chance! *I love you!* I never meant to *hurt* you! *Please* give me a chance to prove to you that I'm

still the *same person*. *Please* let me show you how much I *love* you. *I'm begging you, Sir. Please!"*

I shook my head, and said, *"I'm sorry*, but I just can't see how we can get past this. This wasn't a simple little lie. This was a *major* deception, *months* in the making. Your original intent was to expose me as a phony; *to make a fool of me.* Frankly, I don't know how I could ever trust you again. We can never go back to what we *thought* we had, because what we had was a *lie*. I'm sorry, Valerie. *Goodnight*."

I did my very best to forget about her, and had done a pretty good job of it in the course of the next few months. Then a major storm hit the east coast and dropped a large a tree on her trailer, *crushing it* with her *still inside.* She crawled out of the wreckage and, standing in the pouring rain outside of her collapsed home, called *me* to ask me what she should do. And I *told* her what to do. I found her temporary shelter. I told her what agencies to call. I helped to track down her dogs, which had run off into the stormy night. I helped her to find funding for an eight week stay at a local hotel, and for her eventual move to a new place, closer to her daughter and her grandchildren. I did this because I have a compulsion to *help* people to the best of my ability, *not* because I had any expectation that things could ever go back to the way they were with her.

Several months went by. I helped her to find an affordable and decent apartment. She quit smoking, cut way down on her drinking, and began eating healthier. She lost over 50 pounds, and was looking 10 years younger. She kept trying to tell me that she was doing it all for *me*. I always replied, *no*, she needed to be doing it *for herself.* Eventually, she asked me if I would ever forgive her for her grand deception. I told her that I already *had* forgiven her, but that I would never be able to trust her again, and that things would never go back to the way they were between us in those initial months of our *phony relationship.*

She had an emotional *melt-down*. She cried. She begged. She cajoled. She tried every conceivable argument, every possible angle. She so *desperately* wanted to somehow turn back the hands of time. When nothing *else* worked, she lashed out in a fit of anger and left a message for me on my phone, *threatening* me. I saved the message for the police, and I blocked her phone number. I then sent her a short email which said, "You would do well to remember who you are dealing with here. I'm a combat veteran of three shooting wars. I *don't* scare easily. And you *definitely don't want to fuck with me."*

In retrospect, this was probably *not* the smartest thing I've ever done. I later learned that she used that email to claim that it was *me* who was threatening *her*. And, unfortunately, she made that claim in a *suicide note*, just before taking her own life.

Frankly, I initially believed that the reports of her death were just another one of her *deceptions,* perhaps a sick plea for attention or desperate attempt at revenge. It wasn't until I'd personally spoken on the phone with the *mortician* that I was *truly* convinced. She had, indeed, decided to leave this world cursing and blaming *me*.

You may now consider me a convert to the notion that *no good deed goes unpunished.*

Was Valerie a Warrior Princess Submissive, as she believed? I'll let *you* be the judge.

A Warrior Princess Submissive does not typically pursue activities that they *suck* at.
Valerie sucked at being honest. *And* at being a submissive.

A Warrior Princess Submissive under-promises and over-delivers.
Valerie over-promised, and under-delivered.

A Warrior Princess Submissive uses guile and stealth to *protect* her Dom.
Valerie used guile and stealth *against* her Dom.

A Warrior Princess Submissive sometimes suffers from Imposter Syndrome.
Valerie *was* an *actual* imposter.

A Warrior Princess Submissive is ultra-competent at practically all she does.
Valerie was barely competent at *anything* she did.

A Warrior Princess Submissive is self-sufficient and doesn't require a rescuer.
Valerie was highly dysfunctional, very dependent, and in constant need of rescuers.

A Warrior Princess Submissive is a crusader who believes in right and wrong.
Valerie was an *amoral relativist* whose ends justified the means.

A Warrior Princess Submissive is a *winner*, and almost always comes out *on top.*
A Warrior Princess Submissive *doesn't* take her own life.

Xena: You're gonna cut your throat *and* jump?
That's a bit *overdoing* it don't you think?

(Xena the Warrior Princess, Episode 1.05)

Ares: No. Life isn't worth living. It's to be taken,
and beaten, and wrestled, and formed in your image.
That's where the meaning lies. In what you can twist
life into. For those who just endure life, yeah it is a very
nasty joke. But for those who form it with their will,
the joke is on those who get in the way.
Xena: I *must* be crazy.
You're beginning to make sense.

(Xena the Warrior Princess, Episode 3.01)

Chapter 6: Her Motivation

Why does the Warrior Princess Submissive do what she does? What provides her a reason for getting up in the morning? What sustains her through each day, many of which are characterized by a continuing series of real and exhausting battles? In this chapter we'll try to answer those questions, since knowing *why she does it* is just as important as knowing *what* she does, and *how* she does it. If we are to understand the Warrior Princess Submissive, we must understand what motivates her.

Perhaps quite fittingly for a *warrior*, the acronym "SPAR" may be a useful mnemonic to help us remember the four major reasons the Warrior Princess Submissive is the person she is. SPAR stands for *Service, Perfection, Affiliation, and*

Righteousness. There are, of course, many many compelling reasons for the Warrior Princess Submissive's chosen path, but most of these motivations fall under one or more of these four categories. Let's take a look at them, each in turn.

Service

Service is typically a big part of *any* submissive's life. That should come as no surprise to anyone. The Warrior Princess Submissive, however, takes the concept of service to a *whole new level.*

A typical submissive lives to serve. She likely grew up believing that service to the people you care for is *how you express your love* for them. It had little or nothing to do with relationship dynamics, sex, kink, or anything anywhere near that complicated. It is a simple, sweet principle of love: If you care for someone, you *do nice things* for that person. It makes you feel better, it makes him feel better, and it makes the world - or at least your little corner of it - a better place for a time.

Some of us may have seen this principle at work as we were growing up, demonstrated by our *parents*. Nothing speaks to the principle of service like a mother's love and spirit of sacrifice for her husband and children. Others may not have been so lucky, but may still regard this beautiful principle as *the* ultimate standard for how one expresses his or her love for another.

The Warrior Princess Submissive does more than simply express her love for her *partner* by way of service. The Warrior Princess Submissive expresses her love of country, high principles, faith, social justice, the oppressed, wildlife and the environment, or even humanity in general through her service. She sacrifices her time, resources, and energy as a measure of her ardor and commitment to these causes.

It is not uncommon to find the Warrior Princess Submissive working as a relentlessly energetic *volunteer* for her church, her causes, her politics, or other pursuits. These undertakings, especially when coupled with her *uber*-competence, strong moral compass, leadership abilities, and her superb organizational skills make her a force to be reckoned with in any endeavor she chooses. The downside to this fierce devotion to service is the fact that she often loses a necessary focus upon her own needs and welfare. Not only will she give you the shirt off her back if she thinks you need it, she'll give you her rent money, her family heirlooms, and even the last loaf of bread in her pantry.

Perfection

The Warrior Princess Submissive is, in one very fundamental way, a walking *oxymoron*. She has a deep-seated and sincere need to be *perfect*, yet perfection isn't possible. Her earnest desire to reach this unattainable goal can often lead her to *push* herself physically, emotionally, intellectually, recreationally, and sometimes even *sexually* well beyond the limits of what would typically be considered prudent.

This process of *perfecting herself* and her sense of service are the driving forces behind the Warrior Princess Submissive's *uber*-competence and expertise in her chosen endeavors. "Good enough" *isn't* good enough for her. She strives to be the *best* at what she does, whether it's in her career, her politics, her faith, or even her recreational activities. This is the person who doesn't mind losing at chess or at Scrabble, because she knows it makes her a *better player*.

If she is active in the BDSM lifestyle, she *craves* the chance to learn about new techniques, toys, and play-activities. She avidly reads books, articles, online discussion groups and social media to absorb as much knowledge as she can. She volunteers to be the rope bunny at a local Shibari demonstration, or the spankee for an impact-play class. She naturally gravitates towards and establishes relationships with individuals who have a great deal of knowledge of and experience in the lifestyle. *Why?* It's not just because they're fun or fascinating people. It is because she is driven to be the best possible practitioner of the BDSM arts she can be, and to *be* the best, she feels she must learn from the *best*.

Affiliation

Affiliation is important to the Warrior Princess Submissive. It is one of the unintended consequences of a lifetime of *stealth*. When you invest that much time, energy, and emotion into creating a public persona that contrasts significantly with a core character trait, the predictable result is a palpable sense of alienation. It is *unavoidable*. I've heard Warrior Princess Submissives refer to this phenomenon as a *protective wall*, the *moat* around their castle, or the outer layers of their *onion*. Whatever they call it, it serves but one purpose. It is their solution to maintaining the integrity and functionality of their *stealth apparatus*.

Getting over those walls, through that moat, or inside that onion is a task that is nearly impossible for the average person she meets. In fact, the Warrior Princess Submissive tends to believe that it is, in fact, *actually* impossible, because she has encountered *so many average persons*. She has managed to convince herself that it is absolutely impossible, and is invariably completely *bewildered* when someone simply breezes through her defenses as if they weren't there. Admittedly, this is *not* a task that is easily accomplished. It *can* be done, and we will cover wooing the Warrior Princess Submissive in an upcoming chapter.

My point is this: Getting close to a Warrior Princess Submissive, whether it is as a friend, colleague, or lover, is an *exceedingly rare thing*. She knows this better than *anyone*. Consequently, when she becomes your friend, colleague, or lover, she typically treasures that affiliation above practically *all else*. She isn't just a loyal friend; she is a steadfast, reliable, and devoted friend. She isn't the kind of friend who limits herself to just giving you the shirt off of her back... she's the kind of friend who would give you her own *bone marrow* or a *kidney* if you needed it. She is a *one-of-a-kind* friend.

Enjoy her friendship; bask in her devotion; benefit from that loyalty. But don't ever, *ever*, take it for granted. *Baaaad juju. Trust* me on this one.

Righteousness

The Warrior Princess Submissive has a finely honed sense of right and wrong that sometimes *transcends* simple or stark morality by venturing into the realm of *righteousness*. Where that dividing line lies for certain, I can't tell you. But I *can* tell you that her unique sense of righteousness is closely aligned with her crusading nature. It's one thing to be right, another thing entirely to adopt a *moral imperative* and embark upon a crusade. It's a little like the difference between a medieval knight *acknowledging* Jerusalem as the "Holy Land" versus setting off on his horse to *recapture* it for the church.

The Warrior Princess Submissive's moral paradigm may not necessarily align perfectly with society's prevailing notions of the same, but it *is* an integral part of who she is and one of her primary motivators. Be forewarned, however, about how you will be perceived by her through her *righteousness prism*.

She probably won't *judge* you by the same criteria that she uses to judge herself, but don't let that lull you into a false sense of complacency. This is only because she sets a higher bar for *herself* than she does for *you*. The fact that she doesn't pass moral judgment against you should *never* fool you into thinking that *she won't do battle with you.* Not only *will* she do battle with you if she discovers that you're fighting for the other side, but she will *relish* the fight and wants to drink your blood in the tragic aftermath of your inglorious defeat.

She will enthusiastically do battle with you, *not* necessarily because she thinks you are *evil*, but for the same reason that soldiers have *always* fought their enemies: because they *must be defeated.* For her, it's nothing personal, *but you're going down anyway.*

Motivated

Perhaps mentioning that the Warrior Princess Submissive is *highly motivated* will seem just a tad redundant here, but we would be remiss if we failed to acknowledge her extraordinary *degree* of motivation in all that she does. Most of her friends would probably describe her as *driven.* As far as they are concerned, she works too hard, cares too much, studies too seriously, plays too enthusiastically, fears too little, and dances as if no one is watching. For lack of a word that adequately describes this singular character trait, her friends and associates will often describe her as *intense*. It's a very accurate description.

Her intensity often surprises and mystifies the people within the Warrior Princess Submissive's circle of associates. They will occasionally forget how *deeply* she feels and believes in her causes and, as a result, suddenly find themselves being pummeled in a debate that they hadn't expected, nor wanted. Adopting the role of devil's advocate in any pertinent debate with a Warrior Princess Submissive can be a risky, yet fascinating, exercise in plumbing the depths of her subject-matter knowledge and passion. Just be prepared to defend your position with a commensurate level of understanding and intensity, or risk being humiliated for daring to assume an opposing stance, even temporarily or for the sake of discussion. The *good* news is, she may thrash you mercilessly for disagreeing with her, but she usually doesn't think any less of you, as long as you put up a good fight. In fact, if you put up a *great* fight (remember, it isn't your *volume* or *bullheadedness* she admires, but your *persuasion*) you just might pique her *interest!*

And *that*, my friends, can be a wild ride, *indeed.*

My Two Cents: The Wild Ride

I've told this story to many of my friends over the past few decades, and the inevitable incredulity on their faces has trained me to always preface it with, *"This is a true story."* It is not only true, but it is a little bit *sad*, and it is a tale that is seminally pertinent to whom and what I subsequently became in later years.

Even *I* couldn't make up a story *this* crazy. I usually change the names in my stories in order to spare my friends from any embarrassment, and myself from the resulting grief that comes with that. I'm not even going to change any of the names in *this* one, because I really do think the subject of this story deserves to finally learn *the rest of the story* for herself. Perhaps I'll send her a copy of the book, once it's released.

Or... maybe *not*. I'll get back to you on that.

I was 26 years old when I met Sue, my first Warrior Princess Submissive and a beautiful, *brilliant,* 19-year old brunette during a short break in my twenty-year military career. After just four years of service, I had somehow managed to convince my silly self that I needed to get out of the army and go back to work in the *real* world, where people aren't always telling you *what to do*. (Yes, I was once really *that* stupid.) I became a restaurant manager in Burbank, California, because managing a crew of prima donna cooks, know-it-all bartenders, and PMSing waitresses is just like leading a platoon of soldiers, right? *Sure* it is.

Sue was a shift supervisor who artfully managed an army of mostly poorly-trained waitresses. She was a natural leader, one of my brightest and most capable employees, and we quickly developed a fun, flirty friendship that went from coffee after work to *"What should we name our children?"* in about 6.2 seconds *flat*. She was a free spirit, an energetic force to be reckoned with, and - *surprise* - a submissive.

I was in constant *awe* of her intellect, her technical know-how, her leadership skills, and even her competitive nature, which she handily demonstrated by trouncing me regularly at Scrabble *and* at racquetball. When I met her mother, her *mother* kicked my ass at Scrabble, *too.* That apple didn't fall far from the tree.

Just a few weeks after our first cup of coffee together, we found ourselves in the middle of a particularly aggravating work shift at the restaurant. Remember, I was the *restaurant manager;* she was a shift supervisor. In the midst of all the chaos, I turned to her in exasperation and said, *"Screw this!* Would you like to run away to Hawaii with me?" To my surprise, her immediate response was, "*Sure!* But only if you're *serious* about this."

I *was*. Later that night, I collared her with a chain bearing my *army dog-tags* and the following morning (to the mortification of the restaurant owner) we both turned in our letters of resignation. I sold most of my possessions, placed the rest of my stuff in storage, and within two weeks we were on a jumbo-jet headed for sunny Honolulu. Within a few weeks of our arrival, we each had decent jobs and shared a nice little top-floor efficiency apartment in the center of Waikiki, just one block from the beach. Life was good.

Sue was always ultra-competent and highly competitive in everything that she did, and the time we spent in Hawaii was no different. She excelled at her job and soon developed a wide social circle of friends and admirers. One of them was a pretty and very talented girl named *Taige.*

Taige was a singer in a band that played at the nightclub where Sue worked. Sue gushed about Taige for weeks, until she finally worked up the courage to invite her over one evening, after work. The chemistry between the three of us was immediate, and the three of us bonded over an evening of cheap wine and good conversation. Later in the evening, having run out of wine and feeling much too lazy to go downstairs to buy more, we switched to *tequila*. In retrospect, it's pretty easy to see where that was a really *bad* decision.

Eventually, the three of us ended up dozing in a puppy-pile, and all was well with the world until Sue abruptly sat up and said she needed some fresh air. She excused herself to go out onto the balcony or, as Hawaiian folk prefer to call it, the lanai. Ten minutes passed before Taige said, "Maybe we should check on Sue."

We got up to do just that, but when we pulled back the curtain to the lanai, we were shocked to see *no sign* of Sue. Our first impulse was to think that perhaps she had somehow gone over the safety rail, and peered down at the swimming pool and concrete deck five floors below. Still, *no Sue.* We were completely dumbfounded, and beginning to panic. *Where in the world could she be?*

Just then, there was a knock at the door and I opened it to find a police officer standing there. He asked, "Do you know anything about the girl who fell off the top of this building?" We both reacted with shock and dismay, and ran down the five flights of stairs to where she was laying on the sidewalk in front of the building on the busiest street in Waikiki.

We later learned from the details of the police investigation that she had climbed from our lanai *up onto the roof* of the five story building. Unknown to me, she'd done this before on a regular basis as a way to find an urban island of peace and solitude in the center of a busy tourist mecca that never slept.

On this particular evening, she'd felt nauseous because of the alcohol, but didn't want us to think of her as *fragile* or as a *lightweight*. She had a *reputation* to preserve. She was hard-core *competitive,* even in her *tequila consumption.* To avoid showing us any sign of weakness or imperfection, she climbed from the lanai onto the rooftop, where she discretely vomited. Then, she made her near-fatal mistake. She tried to climb back down *the wrong side of the building.*

Witnesses reported seeing her dangling from the edge of the rooftop for a few moments, before she attempted to swing like Spiderman onto a nearby ledge. She missed, and fell five floors to the pavement below. Luckily, her life was spared when she struck an aluminum awning support pole on her way down, bending the aluminum pole and slowing her descent in the process. Now, there she was, lying on the pavement, bleeding, with several broken bones, and in a severe state of shock.

Surprisingly, she was still conscious. I tried to comfort her while we anxiously waited on the ambulance that the police officer assured us was surely on its way. I held her hand and told her not to worry, that Taige and I were there for her, that the ambulance was coming, and that she was going to be okay. She looked up at me in her shock and delirium and said, "Nooooo! I don't want *you*. I need Bobby here! Someone get *Bobby*."

I looked at Taige in total confusion and asked, "Who is *Bobby?*" She shrugged and replied, "I think she means one of the guys at work." Since Taige was hovering on the verge of hysteria herself, I decided this was probably not a good time to learn more about him. I asked, "Do you know how to get hold of him?" She shook her head emphatically *no.*

The ambulance arrived, and Sue was quickly placed on a gurney and loaded into the back. We were told to meet the ambulance at the hospital. As the heavy rear doors were closed, I could still hear Sue calling out from within the ambulance in her delirium, "Where's Bobby? *Why isn't Bobby here?"*

Sue was in the hospital for about five days. She'd suffered a concussion, a broken clavicle, broken arm, broken leg, and a few bruised and broken ribs. Neither Taige nor the mysterious Bobby ever came to visit Sue in the hospital. I doubt Sue ever recalled mentioning him, and I never did ask her about him. I didn't feel a need to. Some sort of switch in my head or my heart got flipped that night and suddenly, like a light bulb going dark, I simply no longer cared. I hadn't experienced jealousy that day. No, it was *worse* than that. I had simply and suddenly become painfully aware of my *utter irrelevancy.*

Not long afterwards, Sue was on a plane back to California, where she would recuperate with the help and support of her family. I saw her just once more, about a year later, as I passed through California on my way to a new job in Washington D.C. Even though we felt like awkward *strangers* to one another, she was still wearing my army dog tags on a chain around her neck. She asked if I wanted them back. I said *no*.

I learned a couple of extremely painful lessons that night on the sidewalk in Waikiki and in my subsequent late-night introspective thoughts. Relationships - *especially* D/s, poly relationships with *Warrior Princess Submissives* - are often more complex, surprisingly fragile, and far more *dangerous* than you might think. She will do practically *anything* to preserve the magic of her carefully constructed public persona. She may, in fact, *love* you; she may *want* you, but she will rarely admit to ever *needing* you. Falling in love with a Warrior Princess Submissive is definitely *not for the faint of heart.*

On the *bright* side, today Sue is happily married to a successful and highly respected mental health professional who specializes in relationship counseling in north Texas.

Over thirty years have passed and, *no,* we've not stayed in touch.

Sometimes, late at night, I wonder if she still has my dog tags.

Rhein Maiden: What magic has made Xena into
such a noble creature, that she would give
up the power of the Rheingold?
Xena: (looks at Gabrielle and smiles)
It wasn't magic.

(Xena the Warrior Princess, Episode 6.9)

Chapter 7: Total Power Exchange

Total Power Exchange (TPE) is one of those concepts that has been kicking around the BDSM lifestyle for decades, with varying degrees of popularity. One of the difficulties associated with understanding TPE is the fact that most D/s relationships - at least to the casual observer - feature a power exchange that may be *asymmetrical* in nature. To the average person, it may seem as if the submissive has ceded all or most of her power to her Dominant, but it isn't always apparent what power has passed in the *other* direction, from Dominant to submissive.

There is obviously *something* being mutually exchanged in these relationships, but what is it, exactly? For many, it's difficult to understand this notion that power is somehow being exchanged in both directions.

One of the things that can complicate our understanding of this exchange is the fact that, quite often, we are talking about *two completely different relationship dynamics*. For the most part, a D/s dynamic governs the emotions and sense of personal fulfillment in a long-term, committed, and loving D/s relationship. Conversely, a BDSM dynamic typically governs play activity and the physical, kinky interactions with our mates and play partners.

The notion of Total Power Exchange becomes a tremendously useful tool for understanding the true dynamic that exists between a Warrior Princess Submissive and her Dominant. It is entirely possible to understand most of the *other* types of D/s relationship dynamics without having any awareness or understanding of TPE. In fact, the great majority of Dominants and submissives thrive in healthy D/s relationships without giving TPE even a moment of thought.

Why is TPE so important, then, to a *Warrior Princess Submissive's* relationship dynamic? I'll reveal the answer to that question later in this chapter, after we've honed our understanding of TPE by discussing it in terms of *authority* and *empowerment*.

Power vs. Authority

One reason for the general lack of clarity on this issue may be that there are many different ways we can define power. There is even some controversy over the question of whether something can be considered real power if it isn't exercised or exploited. Some people believe that it isn't so much power that is exchanged in TPE, as it is *authority*. The intrinsic difference between power and authority can best be explained thusly: If we were talking about a car, then power would be what was under the hood. Exercising that power would mean taking the car out for a spin. Having the *authority* to do so might involve a driver's license, possessing the keys, or having the title and registration.

In a long-term, committed D/s relationship, both power and authority are exchanged to an exponentially greater degree than in any short-term, uncommitted BDSM play scenario. The reasons for this should be fairly obvious but, to the casual observer, the true nature of the two way exchange may not be. It may be easy to see the authority that a submissive grants to her Dominant to exercise power over her life. It's also easy to see that, even though her Dominant may be exercising that power, the submissive always retains the power and authority to revoke it at will, at any time. Additionally, she typically retains the power or ability to do for herself what she has granted her Dominant the authority to do; she simply chooses not to exercise that power.

Consider the submissive who may be perfectly capable of managing her own household budget, but has *ceded* the authority to do so to her Dominant. Another example is the submissive who may be required to get permission from her Dominant to have an orgasm – any orgasm – even though the power to bring herself to orgasm has always been there, and *always will be*. In these two examples, the *power* is retained even as the *authority* is given."

Empowerment

As part of my research for "Domination & Submission," I surveyed a number of submissives, and asked them, "How are you empowered by your D/s relationship dynamic?" The responses I received were *fascinating* and revelatory. I had always instinctively known that, as a result of *healthy* D/s relationship dynamics, submissives were *empowered.* But, frankly, up to that point I hadn't given a whole lot of thought to listing the many *ways* they could be empowered.

Some of the responses I received included the following:

Empowered to Let Go

I've always found it curious that this particular aspect of TPE is often overlooked by those who attempt to dissect the D/s relationship dynamic as a *true and symmetrical* exchange of power. I sometimes explain my unique take on this subtle form of empowerment by using something I call "the millionaire analogy."

When we see a millionaire who doesn't have to worry about *the little things* that the rest of us mere mortals do, we think of them as being very *powerful*. When Bill Gates says, "I'll let my *assistant* take care of that," or "talk to my *lawyer*," we tend interpret that as an obvious exercise of *power*.

When a submissive says, "I let my *Dominant* handle such matters," or "talk to my *Master,"* she is quite often accused of being a *doormat*. A submissive who delegates the authority to do such things to her Dominant does not do so because she is *incapable* of doing them for *herself.* She does it because it makes her *and* her Dominant *happier*. And unlike the millionaire, she doesn't even have to pay him to do it. So which is more powerful? The millionaire, who has to *pay* someone to do things for him? Or the submissive, who simply has to *allow* it?

Empowered to Transcend Self-limitations

When I was a kid, I was taught that, according to the laws of physics, a bumble bee isn't supposed to be able to fly. The purported lesson to be learned, of course, was that no one ever taught the bumble bee the laws of physics, *and so he flies anyway!* It was a very cool story; one that inspired me as I was growing up to do a *lot* of supposedly impossible things later in life.

Too bad it's a lie. Bumble bees don't really break *any* of the laws of physics, unless you're attempting to apply the principles of *fixed-wing aerodynamics* to *oscillating, flexible, biological aerofoils.* The persistent myth that bumble bees shouldn't be able to fly was given wings *(ouch!)* in a book entitled, "Le Vol des Insectes," which was published in 1934 by French entomologist Antoine Magnan. His calculations turned out to be completely wrong, but that hasn't stopped *bzillions* of school kids from being inspired by his bad math, as *I* was. And the second part of the fable, the part that claims that bumble bees can only fly because they don't know the laws of physics seems just a tad *chauvinistic* to me. There's really *no way* of knowing exactly what may be going on in those little bee brains, is there? Personally, I'd pit a bumble bee's understanding of the physics of flight against *mine* any day.

As part of a *healthy* D/s relationship dynamic, a Dominant may teach, mentor, or guide his submissive in ways that take her beyond what she *believes* are her own limitations. Each time she is directed to do something she would *not normally do on her own*, particularly if it is for her own self-development, education, personal growth, or happiness, she is empowered.

Empowered With Self-confidence

When it comes to loving D/s relationships, the *three little words* mostly likely to have a significant, positive, and lasting impact on your partner's well-being is probably *"I love you."* Once we venture beyond that simple three-word endearment, however, the competition gets much stiffer. If I had to predict a winner in the *four little words* category, I'd choose *"I believe in you."*

When a Dominant *believes* in his submissive, she eventually grows to believe in *herself*. That sort of empowerment is *priceless* beyond measure, and almost always bears sweet fruit.

Such empowerment doesn't just matter for *submissives*, either. During the seven months that it took to write "Domination & Submission," I became so intently focused on finishing the project that I lost sleep, missed meals, and even my health and finances suffered. There were plenty of times, when I seriously wondered if I'd made the right decision to become a full-time writer. *One* of my relationship partners, though *initially* very supportive of my efforts to make it as an author, soon became discouraged and bitter about my decision to leave the corporate rat race. To be fair, going from highly-paid corporate hack to starving writer was a bit of a culture shock for *me, as well.* Before long, she was making it a point to ask almost daily, *"When are you going to go out and get a real job?"* My reply was always, "Never! This *is* my job." She would typically counter with, *"No one* is going to buy your *stupid book.* Go out and find a *real job!"*

My *other* relationship partner at the time was certainly feeling the pinch, *too.* We had far less time together than we were accustomed to, and we were *both* suffering profoundly from severely strained finances. To make matters even worse, my deteriorating health and mood were beginning to seriously undermine my normally-unshakeable self-confidence. *Her* approach, even during the lowest of the low times, was to consistently tell me, *"I believe in you!"* Even when *I* didn't believe in *myself, she* believed in me.

Since then, the book has become a *number one* Amazon best-seller in multiple categories, and *one* of those women has become a *former* relationship partner. I'll give you just two guesses *which.*

Empowered by Trust and Knowledge

At a place called *Tel Tzora,* in the Judean hills of Israel, there is a tomb which is purported to be the final resting place of Samson, hero of the Old Testament's Book of Judges. Whether it *truly* is his tomb, or whether he ever existed *at all*, is a matter of conjecture and debate. Even so, most people at least cursorily know the story of Samson and Delilah, whether or not they believe it. Just in case you're one of the few who doesn't know the story, here's the Cliff notes version.

Samson was granted supernatural strength by God, and had only two known weaknesses: *bimbos and haircuts.* His super-human feats included ripping apart a lion with his bare hands, slaying a thousand philistines with the jawbone of an ass, and destroying the Temple of Dagon, just to name just a few. His ultimate undoing came at the hands of his lover, Delilah, who was bribed by the Philistines with 1100 pieces of silver to learn and reveal Samson's *other* weakness. After gullibly believing and proving false several explanations that Samson provided to her, Delilah finally learned his *real* weakness and orders a servant to shave his head and who knows what else.

Once he is robbed of his strength by the mercenary bimbo *twat-waffle* he loves, Samson is captured by the Philistines, brutally blinded, and forced to work (*clumsily*, I'm guessing) as a slave in a granary. Eventually, his *dumb-ass* captors forget all about the need to give Samson regular haircuts, and stupidly allow his hair to grow long again. This happens just in time for a big shindig at the Temple of Dagon, where the plan is to put Samson on public display and humiliate him. Instead, Samson uses his extraordinary strength to bring the massive temple down on everyone in attendance, including himself, and everyone dies unhappily ever after. *The End.*

The story of Samson and Delilah aptly demonstrates how a Dominant may - for better or for worse - entrust his submissive with the sure knowledge of how to *destroy* him. A *worthy* submissive will never *exercise* that knowledge in such a way, but knows in her heart of hearts that she is indeed *empowered* by it.

Empowered by Authority

When a submissive speaks for her Dominant (with his certain knowledge and consent) she situationally and temporarily borrows a portion of his power to accomplish a specific task or mission. The influence that can be wielded in the exercise of such authority cannot be underestimated. Whenever I find myself moderating an online group, forum, or chat room, I always place a submissive in charge of booting and/or banning the trouble-makers, most of whom invariably turn out to be clueless, *wanna-be Dominants*. It pleases me *immensely* to see a pompous, full-of-himself buffoon of a Tin Pot Dom get *reamed* by a subbie with the authority to put him in his place.

Empowered by Synergy

Synergy is defined as a process by which the sum of the parts equals more than the aggregate of the parts, when considered individually. It can be loosely thought of as the process of making *two plus two equal five.* Working together and taking advantage of the synergy in their relationship dynamic, a Dominant and his submissive can and often do accomplish great things that *neither* could have done *alone*. It is, in a word, the power of *teamwork.* This book, *itself*, is a testament to this principle.

These aspects of power exchange are present, to one degree or another, in just about every D/s relationship dynamic. Your particular relationship may or may not manifest them *all*, but if it is a *healthy* relationship, it will surely exhibit *some* of them.

My Two Cents: Empowerment

"Thank you, Master," Kitten *mewed,* as we cuddled on the couch after watching Mystery Science Theater's version of the 1964 sci-fi movie *"The Atomic Brain."*

I inwardly chuckled at the thought of being *thanked* for that dreadful movie about a mad scientist who works for a pugnacious little old lady *body-snatcher*. It's one of those movies that is *so awful, it's funny.*

"No, not for the silly *movie*, Master!" she giggled and continued, "I meant... for... *everything."*

"Ahhh," I said, nodding sagely as if I had even the tiniest clue. "Well, you're *welcome*... for... ermmm... everything!" Long, silent pause, still nodding. Finally, unable to contain myself any longer, I chortled, "Okay, what the *hell* are we talking about?"

Kitten laughed, and replied, "I meant... thank you... for making me a stronger person. For helping me to get my priorities straight. For teaching me how to stand up for myself, and not be pushed around anymore. For showing me how to focus my attention and energy on positive things, instead of the negatives. For teaching me how to stay calm, when I would normally freak out. For surrounding me with good people who actually *care* about me and aren't trying to exploit me, for the first time in my life. For being my safe haven in the storm. For loving me the way that you do!"

Whoa, I thought. I wasn't sure a simple *"you're welcome"* was going to suffice as an adequate comeback to all *that!* I kissed Kitten gently on the forehead and said, "I didn't accomplish any of that, Kitten. *You did*. I'm *very* proud of you. And I'm not the *only* one. A *lot* of people have noticed wonderful changes in you over the past several months, and *they're* all very proud of you, too."

She wiggled and mewed, and said, "I *feel* different. I'm much more *confident*. I'm *happier*. I like where I am now, and where I am going. I now have the courage to walk away from someone who is being a jerk... or to walk up to someone I've just met, and ask her out to coffee. I could never have done *either,* just six months ago! It's... it's... *kind of exhilarating!*"

I smiled. "I *know*, Kitten. That's the way it's *supposed* to work. Frankly, it doesn't always work out as planned, but when it *does*, it's truly a beautiful thing to see *and* to experience. That's my job... to give you the guidance, the resources, the motivation, and the room to grow into the person that you were always *meant* to be. I just pointed you in the right direction; *you* did the hard part. I can't say it enough: *I'm proud of you!"*

Kitten *beamed.* She *mewed* happily, as she hugged me tightly and licked my cheek. We wallowed in our little oasis of warm-fuzziness for another ten minutes or so, before returning to normality and the mundane daily tasks at hand.

"So. Are you all done with that *Calculus* homework of yours?" I asked, with an evil grin.

Kitten still swears that her response - a guttural sound that emanated from deep within her - was, in actuality, a *purr*. It sounded a lot more like a *growl* to me, but I suppose I'll never know for certain.

Gabrielle: So, what's this Petracles like?
Xena: He's a warlord. He's an ambitious,
ruthless,
dominating, conniving liar. He'll say anything
he can
to get a woman to fall for him, and then once
he has her, he uses her.
Gabrielle: So, you've met.
Xena: We were to be *married.*

(Xena the Warrior Princess, Episode 1.14)

Chapter 8: The Switchy Feminist

Every lifestyle choice is, at its core, *a quest for happiness*. Life is, after all, too short to spend it *unhappy*. To that end, we should be very cautious about allowing ourselves to be defined or labeled by our *physiology*, our *circumstances*, our *careers*, or even our leisure-time *distractions*.

What truly defines us is how we feel and relate to the people that we care about. Let's take a look at a few examples.

If we were talking about *gender*, we would not be defined by what sex organs happen to be between our legs, but by *how we feel about them*. Just because I happen to have a penis and testicles doesn't necessarily mean I *must identify as a male*. If I relate to my partner as a *female*, then *that* is what defines me as a person. *That is who I am.* The *clothes* that I wear to work each day or when I am out in public do not define me. What *other* people think about who or what I am does not define me. I am defined solely by how I feel and how I relate. *Period.*

Similarly, we should not *necessarily* be defined solely on the basis of *what we do* in the fetish lifestyle. The mere fact that someone is proficient as a *Top* does not make that person a *Dominant,* and being a *bottom* does not automatically make him a *submissive*.

Being a Dominant or a submissive is a consequence and function of *how you feel* and how you express that in the *dynamic* that exists between you and your loved one(s). Unless and until you have truly been in a loving D/s relationship with a partner, it will be extremely difficult to categorize yourself as either a Dominant or submissive. It would be very much like trying to figure out how proficient you are at *ballroom dancing* without ever having had a real, live *dance partner*.

Many people in the lifestyle - both novices *and* veterans - make the unfortunate mistake of *prematurely* classifying themselves as switches simply as a result of not having experienced a *true D/s relationship* of any real significance up to that point. This is a terrible shame, in my view. Definitively **c**ategorizing oneself as a switch (or as *anything*, really) should only be done after accumulating considerable experience in the lifestyle, getting at least a few deep and lasting D/s relationships under your belt, and after a great deal of reflection and self-exploration. Adopting the label of a "Switch" should never be the result of a "default" classification for those who are simply unsure about their D/s orientation.

Once the issue has been weighed adequately and a decision arrived at to consider oneself a Switch, some thought should be devoted to assessing what *kind* of Switch you might happen to be. *Surprise!* Yes, there *are* several different types of Switches.

Types of Switches

In *Domination & Submission: The BDSM Relationship Handbook,* I presented the case for *eight* distinct contemporary categories of Switches.

They were:

Provisional Switch. A person who has not had sufficient lifestyle or relationship experiences to make a definitive assessment of his *switchiness.*

Dominant-leaning D/s Switch. A person who willfully switches between Dominant and submissive, with a tendency to favor being a Dominant in his *relationship dynamic.*

Submissive-leaning D/s Switch. A person who willfully switches between Dominant and submissive, with a tendency to favor being a submissive in his *relationship dynamic.*

Balanced D/s Switch. A person who willfully switches between Dominant and submissive, without favoring *either* role in his *relationship dynamic*. This is *extremely rare*. There will almost *always* be a preference, irrespective of the ease with which the switch occurs and the joy experienced in each role.

Top-leaning BDSM Switch. A person who willfully switches between *topping* and *bottoming* in his *BDSM-play activities*, and favors the role of a *Top*.

Bottom-leaning BDSM Switch. A person who willfully switches between *topping* and *bottoming* in his *BDSM-play activities*, and favors the role of a *bottom*.

Balanced BDSM Switch. A person who willfully switches between *topping* and *bottoming* in his *BDSM-play activities*, without a preference for either role. This is relatively *rare*.

D/s-BDSM Switch. A person who willfully switches between being a Dominant in his *relationship dynamic* and a bottom in his *BDSM activities*, or conversely, being a submissive in his *relationship dynamic* and a Top in his *BDSM activities*. This category can be difficult to sort out in your own head if you are unable to clearly distinguish between aspects of *who you are*, and *what you do*.

This list deliberately omits a type of switch that I had mentioned in my previous work as being somewhat *archaic*, which was what I termed the *Classic Switch.* The Classic Switch, in decades past, referred to a person who always felt Dominant to *one* gender, yet submissive to *another*. Historically, the predominant manifestation of this dynamic was usually a *woman* who felt *dominant* to other females, and *submissive* to males. Today, however, attributing the mechanics of any relationship dynamic to real or imagined *gender distinctions* has very much fallen out of favor and is probably not very useful to our purposes. Any predisposition to assign *traditional* gender roles to a propensity for switchiness will usually result in an extra-topical debate on *gender bias*, when what we *really* want to talk about here is *switchiness*.

Switch or Switchy Sub?

We've recapped the various categories of switches, at least, as they have been defined in *my* humble estimation. Perhaps we should now return to the question which is at the heart of this chapter: Is the Warrior Princess Submissive a *switch*, or is she simply a *switchy submissive?*

To *further* complicate matters, I'm going to go way out on a limb here and say something that is probably going to infuriate at least a few of my switchy Amazon Princess friends. Here it is: I believe that an Amazon Princess Submissive is invariably going to be the *worst possible judge* of her *own* switchy nature. Here's why I think so.

First, she lacks proper perspective. She's *too close* to it to be able to see it objectively. It's a little like trying to determine for yourself if you have a *sexy butt.* Eventually, we all have to resort to *asking* someone who has a better view of it.

Second, she habitually and quite unconsciously runs her partners and prospective partners through a punishing gantlet that would terrify and bewilder *most* would-be suitors. *She* thinks it's because she is demanding and domineering when, in fact, it's simply because she is incredibly *picky*.

Third, she has the same *blind spot* that most of us do, when it comes to being oblivious to certain character traits in potential partners that should *obviously* make that person a poor choice for a committed relationship. Unfortunately, those traits are usually obvious to just about everyone *except* us. Admit it;

you *know exactly* who and what I am talking about, here. We're talking about that friend of yours who really wants to find a *nice guy*, so she joins the *Death Row Pen Pal Program*. Or the woman who says she can't stand *drunks*, but keeps looking for Mr. Right in the local bars and nightclubs. Or the newbie submissive in Ohio who chooses *Mr. I-Can't Even Spell-BDSM,* who happens to live in *Sri Lanka* and can only chat via Facebook while his local library is open, to be her *Lord and Master*.

Finally, she likely lacks the requisite relationship experience to arrive at an adequate assessment. If she is still seeking her *One*, then she is still drawing an erroneous conclusion from an incomplete data set, and based upon faulty premises.

Of *course* she thinks she is a switch!

At first blush, it would be pretty difficult for anyone to think *otherwise*, would it not? After all, her public persona is extraordinarily dominant, while her relationship dynamic is expressed as a submissive. The contrast, *even for her*, is stark and often terribly confusing. She sometimes finds herself wondering which one of those personas is the *"real"* one. The answer, of course, is that they *both are.* That *doesn't*, however, necessarily make her a switch.

Let's try a little analogy that may help to illustrate my point. Perhaps you are a woman who is the proud parent of one or more wonderful children. That makes you a *mother*, does it not? But are you not *also* a *daughter* to the woman who brought you into the world? Which of those two appellations are you *really?* Mother or daughter? Obviously, you can be *both*. The roles manifest themselves as appropriate and necessary in your life and there really is no compelling reason to have to choose one of these roles as the *"real one."*

You are doing what *most* people do, which is drawing upon each persona as appropriate for the personal relationship dynamic that you enjoy with either your child or your parent. You would probably never consider relating to your child as *her* daughter, nor would you presumably want to relate to your mother as *her* parent (even if it becomes necessary in her declining years). For most of us, the very notion seems ludicrous or unpleasant to have to imagine.

Let's return then, to the premise we put forward at the beginning of this chapter, which was the notion that it isn't *what we do* that defines us, but *how we feel about it.* More to the point, it isn't what we do at work or play that defines our D/s role, it is *how we relate* and express our love in a D/s *relationship dynamic.* And *no*, your participation in a fifteen minute BDSM scene at your local dungeon does not a relationship make, no matter *how* much fun it may have been!

During their childhood and teen years, most women would describe themselves primarily as *daughters*. Then, something wonderful happens, and they become *mothers*. Suddenly, that *relationship dynamic* between this mother and her child becomes *primary* and *paramount*. Has she somehow become any less the daughter to her mom that she always was? No, nothing has changed there, *except the primacy of her relationship dynamic* with her new daughter. As her daughter matures and leaves the nest, perhaps there will be more balance between the two roles. Eventually, her daughter becomes increasingly independent while her mother becomes older, frailer, and requires additional care. When this happens, even the role of a daughter can take on entirely new meaning and responsibilities.

Let's be clear here. Through *all* of this, the *person* hasn't changed. Only her *relationship dynamics* have changed over the course of time.

Now, let's take our little mother-daughter analogy a step further in order to help us understand why the Warrior Princess Submissive often considers herself to be a Switch. Imagine what you *thought* it would be like *to be a mother* when you were *ten years old.* Think about how well you understood what it would truly be like to experience a lifetime of love, loss, joy, sacrifice, hardship, and all the other aspects of being *both* a mother *and* a daughter. Not only does she *not* fully grasp the magnitude and scope of it all, there is absolutely *no way that she could* grasp it.

I'm *not* saying that a Warrior Princess *can't be* a Switch. What I *am* saying is this: It is fairly common for a *Warrior Princess Submissive* to erroneously *believe* that she is a Switch. In my humble estimation, she is not a Switch. She is a *switchy submissive.* I believe this because, as I postulated in a previous chapter, we are defined by *how we relate to our partners.* In the case of a Warrior Princess Submissive, she *always* relates to her partner as a submissive. She is, therefore, a *submissive.* Her *switchiness towards others* is, for the most part, irrelevant to the general thesis of this volume.

In other words, there may *indeed* be such a thing as a *Warrior Princess Switch,* but this book isn't about *her*.

Her Feminism

In addition to being *switchy*, the Warrior Princess Submissive is almost *by definition* a feminist. Why? It is because she has spent her entire life defying the societal stereotypes that often hamstring other women. She has succeeded, often in careers and endeavors that have traditionally been reserved for men. She defies these limitations and expectations instinctively and without fear or trepidation. In fact, she *relishes* it in ways that even she doesn't fully understand, at times.

This doesn't necessarily mean that the Warrior Princess Submissive will always find herself on the political front lines of the feminist fray. Some Warrior Princess Submissives will, indeed, be very active in the feminist movement but the great majority will consider that political crusade much ado about nothing. In their own minds, they have already proven to themselves and to the world that they are forces to be reckoned with, and have demonstrated success in a world that frequently makes women work twice as hard to accomplish the very same things as their male counterparts.

For the Warrior Princess Submissive, her feminism is less about "talking the talk," and more about *"walking the walk."* She doesn't have to wear her feminism on her sleeve; she *exudes it from every pore* and typically demonstrates it in practically everything she does. No, the issue - when it comes to the Warrior Princess' feminism - isn't *whether or not she is a feminist*; it's about how she reconciles her feminism with her *submission* and how she is perceived by those around her. Often, she is quite simply unable to do so *publicly*, which is why she has learned to be *stealthy*.

My Two Cents: The Warrior Princess Switch

I truly wanted to let this particular sleeping dog lie but I also knew, in my heart of hearts, that a large number of my readers simply wouldn't allow it. *Especially* the redheads.

For the record, I honestly believe that the great majority of Warrior Princesses out there are *submissives* at their core. I *will* readily concede that there may, indeed, *also* be some Warrior Princess *Switches* out there, but - *sorry* - this book is about Warrior Princess *Submissives*. I *will*, however - purely for the sake of argument - entertain the theoretical question: *What kind of Switch would a Warrior Princess be?*

If you've made it this far into this book, you know by now that I am an incorrigible *word-maker-upperer.* I am also unafraid, when a data sample fails to conform to any known categorization process, to invent *whole new categories* for it. When the rules no longer fit, rewrite the rules! If existing words fail to describe what you see, invent new ones! The question at hand may force us to resort to just such a strategy.

Let's begin by acknowledging that the Warrior Princess Switch cannot be easily be pigeon-holed into any of the eight categories of Switches listed at the beginning of this chapter. Let's further concede that she doesn't fit the mold of what I've described as a *Classic Switch,* which is someone who *consistently* feels dominant towards one gender while, at the same time, submissive towards another. The *contemporary* definition of a Switch is quite different. It has essentially come to describe someone who changes their D/s or BDSM orientation *at will*, often with the *same person.*

Let's backtrack, for just a moment, to the Warrior Princess *Submissive*. *Classic Switch* may *superficially* describe *her* behavior *before* she finds her *One*, but once she finds Him, *the Classic Switch rules no longer fit* and they are summarily discarded. Typically, once she finds her One, gender becomes entirely *irrelevant* to the Warrior Princess Submissive. In her *new* way of thinking, the world is no longer divided into categories based on gender or any *other* superfluous categorization criterion. For the Warrior Princess *Submissive*, the world is *now* divided thusly: *Him, and Not Him.*

Not so, for the Warrior Princess *Switch*. She switches with *Him*. She switches with *others*. She switches whenever, however, and with *whomever* she pleases. Her propensity to switch may be based on gender, height, bearing, mood, hormones, phases of the moon, the weather, a coin flip, or *nothing at all.* It *could,* in fact, be entirely *random*. Frankly, *that* possibility gives me the *heebie-jeebies.*

No matter how *"in charge"* a Warrior Princess *Submissive* may seem to the entire *world*, there will always be that certain *someone* who can rein her in, keep her grounded, and remind her that she is just as fallible as the rest of us - her *Dominant*. This is *not* the case with a Warrior Princess *Switch*. The typical relationship dynamic with *any* true Switch will almost always be fluid and malleable. The person who she claims as her Dominant *today* may, *tomorrow*, be her *whipping boy*. And remember, she is still a highly competent warrior, a crusader, incredibly stealthy, full of righteousness, and highly motivated. She is accountable to *no one*, other than herself.

How should we categorize the Warrior Princess Switch, if she truly exists?

One word: *Scary*.

Man: Looking for the man of your dreams?
Xena: *Yep*... (Punches him in the stomach.)
You're not him.

(Xena the Warrior Princess, Episode 1.11)

Chapter 9: Wooing Her

Wooing the Warrior Princess Submissive can be a complex and difficult undertaking, as this snippet from the Xena series amply illustrates:

Amazon #1: Well, I'm a virgin and I'm gonna *stay* that way forever!
Xena: Forever is a long time...
Amazon #2: What's it like, being with a man?
Xena: The good news is, it's different every time...the bad news is - it's different every time. You're always hoping for a Greek fire, but sometimes you just get diddly.
Gabrielle: Xena has studied the subject more than I have, but I think she's trying to say that some people are better lovers than others.
Amazon #2: What makes a man a good lover? Being gentle and kind?
Xena (resolutely): *No*.
Gabrielle (dreamily): *Yes*.
Gabrielle (after a while): It's a complicated subject.

(Xena the Warrior Princess, Episode 5.17)

After learning about the Warrior Princess Submissive in the previous chapters, perhaps you are beginning to find yourself as fascinated and attracted to her as *I* am. You may even be thinking that it might be fun, exciting, or worthwhile to pursue some sort of *relationship* with someone you know, who shares many of the most fascinating characteristics of the Warrior Princess Submissive.

If so, this chapter is for *you*.

If, on the other hand, you happen to be someone who is beginning to suspect that *you* are a Warrior Princess Submissive, this chapter may serve to explain a few things about your own perplexing social life which may have puzzled you in the past. Some of those questions may include:

- Why are guys seemingly intimidated by me?
- Should I conceal my intelligence when dating?
- Why do some guys disappear the first time we have a spirited discussion about some important issue of the day?
- Why do I have such a hard time finding someone that I can trust and respect?
- How aggressive should I be in my search for a partner?
- Should I be looking for a Dominant, switch, or submissive as a potential partner?
- To what degree should I attempt to separate my D/s relationship dynamic(s) from my BDSM activities?

The sad truth is, many men truly *are* intimidated by demonstrably strong, intelligent, and competitive women. Curiously enough, women tend to be simultaneously intimidated *and* attracted to men with the same qualities. Stereotypical gender roles seem to have set those particular characteristics aside as being traditionally *male* ones, which explains the confusion and hesitation some males may experience when they unexpectedly encounter them in a *woman.*

This conundrum becomes even more perplexing when the male is a typical *Dominant* seeking a traditional submissive. The Warrior Princess Submissive herself may be uncertain of her own submissive nature, so it is entirely understandable that the Dominant seeking to woo her might be somewhat tentative, himself. If the Dominant has even the tiniest iota of doubt about his own dominance or his D/s relationship skills, he is *doomed.* He will be *eaten alive,* and *not* in a good way.

The Warrior Princess Submissive *isn't* a brat or a pseudo-submissive, but she invariably *will* test the mettle of any prospective suitors *unmercifully.* If you think the standards she has set for *herself* are high, you'll probably suffer *vertigo* from the incredibly high standards that she sets for her prospective *partners.* Any prospective suitor would do well to first take stock of himself and perform a brutal self-evaluation before embarking on this course.

Her Expectations

She expects a *lot* from her prospective mates. Many will step up to be considered and will be found lacking. She is rarely despondent about it or deterred in her quest, however. She knows her *knight* is out there, *somewhere*.

In this quest, just as in her career or social crusades, she is doggedly relentless. She *instinctively* knows that each pretender she eliminates brings her one step closer to the One, and in fact, it is not unusual to hear her use this *exact terminology:* The One. You can almost *hear* the Capitalization as she says it.

So, what is it that the Warrior Princess Submissive seeks in a potential mate?

Fearlessness. Not only must this potential suitor be someone who is *unafraid* of strong, intelligent, and competitive women, he must be someone who is actually *attracted* to them. As odd as it may sound, this quality is relatively rare among the general male population. One would think that it would be less a concern among lifestyle Dominants but, even there, we find a disconcertingly high percentage of males who are either incapable or unwilling to rise to the challenge of an exceptionally capable submissive.

Competency. The Warrior Princess Submissive is extremely good at what she does and, consequently, she typically expects her knight to be similarly *uber*-competent at whatever it is that *he* does. The reason for this is simple. She simply doesn't understand why or how anyone would expend time, energy, and resources to doing something *badly*. It is an entirely foreign concept to her. She's is good at what she does, and expects you to be, too.

Crusader. While her knight doesn't necessarily have to be fighting on the *same side* as the Warrior Princess Submissive, he *does* need to be a fighter, and he had better be damn *good* at it. She may not necessarily ever *agree* with you, but she does have to *respect* you and your positions on the issues. You may find yourselves on opposite ends of the socio-political spectrum, but that's not necessarily a problem as long as you can defend your reasoning competently. You should never fool yourself into thinking you'll ever change her mind, however.

Articulate. She expects you to be able to hold your own in a spirited discussion or debate. She expects you to be able to have your beliefs and assumptions challenged without getting angry or getting your feelings hurt. She wants you to be able to challenge hers, as well, in ways that will make her grow intellectually and to fortify her own positions.

Stimulating. When you help her to grow intellectually or emotionally, you stimulate the Warrior Princess Submissive in ways that are rarely encountered in her day-to-day life. She deals with mundane individuals all day, every day. When you are the one person in a hundred that *stimulates* her, you're *golden.*

Dominant. A Warrior Princess Submissive seeks not just a Dominant; she seeks a *Dominant's Dominant.* There can be no measure of doubt in his mind, nor hers, about his innate capacity to be the *leader* in this relationship dynamic. This is doubly important because of her inherent *switchiness*. Since she can often draw from both ends of the D/s spectrum, she instinctively needs a mate who is firmly grounded at the Dominant end. Additionally, because there are so many Dominants who become wobbly when it comes to being challenged, the Warrior Princess Submissive often seeks out seasoned and highly experienced Dominants as their potential mates. There'll be no *wanna-be* or *role-play* Dominants for her. She'll settle for nothing less than a proven *real deal.*

Separating (or Integrating) BDSM and D/s

In the course of the Warrior Princess Submissive's quest for a mate, she will often be faced with the challenge of integrating (or, conversely, separating) her BDSM activities from her D/s relationship dynamic. To recap what we've stated earlier in this book and in other works, I've always maintained that BDSM is an *activity*, or something that you *do*. D/s, on the other hand, is a *relationship dynamic*; it's how you express your love for your partner. It's where you find your *"happy place."* In light of this, why would the Warrior Princess Submissive need to either integrate or separate her BDSM from her D/s? The answer lies entirely in the degree to which her BDSM and D/s are already balanced adequately.

If, for example, her life revolves heavily around BDSM activities, but she has not yet found a suitable potential mate with whom to establish a stable D/s relationship, then perhaps she needs to integrate the two more efficiently by focusing less on the whips and chains, and more on the *flowers and chocolate.* The flip-side of that situation would be the couple who has focused so exclusively on the D/s dynamic in their relationship, that it exists in a vacuum, without any significant BDSM play. In both of these scenarios, a greater degree of integration between their D/s and BDSM may be warranted.

Conversely, in situations that are muddled or where the lines are blurred, there may exist a need to draw certain distinctions. One example might be a situation where individuals engage in BDSM purely as *play partners* and, as a result, erroneously come to believe that this activity constitutes a true *"relationship."* Using the traditional sex/love analogy, engaging in BDSM play with someone doesn't put you in a relationship with him any more than having *sex* with him does.

A *vanilla* couple may sometimes have to step back to analyze their relationship by asking, "Do we have anything in common other than great sex?" Many couples have made the mistake of mistaking sexual attraction for real love. Likewise, many people make the mistake of confusing BDSM enjoyment with a true D/s relationship dynamic. In those cases, the ability to separate the two becomes paramount.

The Warrior Princess Submissive's ability to recognize these distinctions and make proper use of them in the analysis of her relationships is crucial in her quest for her One. Her innately *switchy* nature already muddies the waters a great deal for her, often in ways she can scarcely comprehend. Add to the mix any confusion of BDSM with D/s, and it makes her task nearly impossible.

Toss Out the Rule Book

Frankly, there are no hard and fast rules for wooing a Warrior Princess Submissive. If you're considering it, the first thing you might want to consider is a good hospitalization plan and adequate life insurance coverage. You might also want to avoid ever actually speaking aloud the word *"wooing"* in her presence.

Trust me on this.

I've actually courted quite a few Warrior Princess Submissives in my long and storied lifetime. After all, she *is* my submissive of choice, all other things being equal. I sometimes think I have survived the process each time simply because I am a short, dorky, half-Asian nerd. In other words, I'm perceived by most people to be *relatively harmless*.

For all of you Dominants who *aren't* lucky enough to be short, dorky, half-Asian nerds, perhaps you can take a page from *The Praying Mantis Relationship Handbook,* now available at *Amazon.bug.*

Courting for praying mantises is *complicated*, which is an understatement of epic proportions. The intrepid male praying mantis, prior to initiating courtship with the female mantis of his choice, purchases a nice burial plot and a sturdy athletic cup on the extreme off-chance that he will survive. The male then performs an energetic courtship dance, the sole purpose of which is to convince the female that he has no rhythm and is far too dorky and/or stupid to be a threat to her in any way.

The female praying mantis, whose mood is typically a curious mixture of *horny* and *bat-shit-crazy-homicidal*, watches this insectoid version of the *chicken dance* with rapt attention and, though intrigued and entertained by his sincerely heartfelt performance, naturally begins to wonder if he *tastes* like chicken. This may, to the casual observer, seem like a totally crazy thing to be thinking in the middle of a courtship dance, but... *hormones*.

Next, the male and the female praying mantises proceed to the next phase of their courtship, which is copulation. *Copulation* is what scientists, nerds, and (apparently) praying mantises call *doing the horizontal hustle.* I won't even try to pretend to know what bugs *think* about during sex, but right about the time the male praying mantis is probably thinking that he's *quite the stud*, the female does something pretty surprising. Yes, even for horny, bat-shit-crazy, homicidal copulating bugs.

Once she has had enough of *copulating*, she moves on to the next phase, which is *masticating*. No, not *masturbating...* masticating. This is a fancy-schmancy word for *chewing*. She chews his head off. And *no*, I don't mean like, *"Why didn't you bring me flowers and chocolate?"* Oh, no. She *literally* bites his head off... and *here's* where it gets *really* interesting:

She eats it.

Unsurprisingly, the unexpected loss of the male's brain does *not* stop him from continuing to have sex with the female. In fact, it *doesn't even slow him down.* Not even a little bit. Scientific studies have actually been conducted to learn more about this bizarre phenomenon and the conclusions they've reached demonstrate what most women have instinctively known most of their lives.

When it comes to sex and courtship, males often think with their *little* heads.

Xena (to an unconscious Draco, lying on the ground):
"I'm sorry, sweetie, that hurt me a lot more than it hurt you.
Sweetie? Did I say *sweetie*? I've never used that word in
my life before! Oh, but he's so *cute*."

(Xena the Warrior Princess, Episode 2.22)

Borias: What would you do if I told you I am in love?
Xena: I'd cut out your sweetheart's throat.
You think I wouldn't?
Borias: *No*, I mean I'm in love with *you*.
Xena: With *me?* Have you lost what's left of your *mind?*
People like you and me don't fall in love...
Not with each *other*, anyway.

(Xena the Warrior Princess, Episode 4.01)

My Two Cents: Wooing Her

I *wish* I could tell you exactly how it should be done. This is about as close as I'll be able to get: *very carefully.*

You should probably count yourself lucky simply to be able to discern whether or not you're making any real progress. You may or may not even realize when you've *succeeded.*

She can be a riddle, wrapped in an enigma, inside a conundrum, rolled in a *frito burrito*. In other words, *a total freaking mystery* to anyone who isn't gifted with mind-reading abilities.

Kylie, a twenty year-old college crusader *and* one of the inspirations for this book, is a fine example of just *how* enigmatic a Warrior Princess Submissive can be. She blogs regularly on a wide variety of topics, to include women's rights, D/s, and polyamory. One day, she sent me a message about something she'd written.

"I'm writing an article about polyamorous relationships," she said. "Would it be alright to mention you? And if so, should I mention you by name, or should I make up a pseudonym for you?"

Frankly, her question caught me somewhat by surprise. We'd only met face to face for the first time a short time earlier, and only a few times since. The aggregate number of hours we'd spent together at this point could probably have been counted on two hands. It was certainly true that I was *smitten* with her, but it would have been presumptuous, indeed, to think that we had much more than a tentative, flirty friendship.

I was definitely intrigued by the prospect of being mentioned in her article about polyamory, so I asked, "What, specifically, are you going to say about me? I suppose the appropriate use of my real name will depend a great deal upon that."

She replied, "It's just a few paragraphs describing our relationship."

"Ooooh!" I said, chuckling, "We're in *relationship?* What *sort* of relationship?"

There followed a discernable pause in our usually swift dialog, during which I imagined the nimble mental gymnastics she *had* to be executing in order to arrive at a sufficiently cryptic and noncommittal response. When it finally came, it was - *for her* - *surprisingly* forthright. She said, "The kind of relationship that is at least important enough to be mentioned in any article about the people I care about and how I relate to them in a polyamorous relationship dynamic!"

I read the sentence carefully a few times over, just to be completely sure that I wasn't misreading or misinterpreting what she'd actually *said*. In the end, I just decided to throw caution to the wind and count it as a *win*.

Xerxes: Who are you and what is your interest in all this?
Xena: My name is Xena. I'm a *problem-solver*.

(Xena the Warrior Princess, Episode 1.11)

Chapter 10: Hope and Salvation

"What do you think of the novel Fifty Shades of Grey?" It's a question I am asked at least a dozen times each day by fans, friends, and associates. My answer is always the same: *Not much.* Never mind, that I rarely read much fiction at *all*, since I generally prefer to read nonfiction works. But seeing my lifestyle mischaracterized as it was in E.L. James' 50 Shades trilogy simply threatens to make my head explode.

The first book of the *Fifty Shades* trilogy was originally written and posted online as a piece of *Twilight* fan fiction entitled *Master of the Universe.* The author, writing under the pen name *Snowqueen's IceDragon*, received a significant amount of negative feedback about the piece due to its graphic sexual nature. Consequently, she removed it from the Twilight fan fiction site, changed the characters' names, and rewrote other portions of the work. She then reposted the refurbished manuscript to her *own* website, 50shades.com, and later to print and e-book.

The rest is, as they say, *history*.

Fifty Shades of Grey has since sold more copies than the entire *Harry Potter* series combined, with book sales exceeding *60 million copies,* and has become one of the best-selling books in history. Just *think* about that for just a moment. The population of the United States of America is slightly over *300 million.* Not the *adult* population... the *entire* population. If we assume that the *adult* population of the U.S. is roughly 240 million, then that would equate to *one copy of Fifty Shades for every four adults in the country.*

I don't know about *you*, but I find that just a little mind-boggling.

I also find it more than just a little concerning. I find it concerning because I believe that the *Fifty Shades* trilogy and the never-ending series of *Fifty Shades* movies that will be produced as a consequence glorify *unhealthy* and *potentially dangerous* BDSM relationships. And by potentially dangerous, I *don't* mean just for the occasionally naive reader who thinks the actual lifestyle is anything like what is portrayed in the books. I think the growing popularity of the Fifty Shades franchise is potentially dangerous *for the lifestyle itself, and for everyone who lives it.*

It should come as no surprise to anyone reading this book that the BDSM lifestyle has come under attack in recent years by an unlikely alliance of militant feminists, religious fundamentalists, and survivors of past physical, sexual, or emotional abuse. Their dogma invariably rests upon one or more of the following pillars, typically delivered to members of the lifestyle in the most condescending way possible:

- You don't really know what you want.

- You are obviously confused or self-deluded.

- You're suffering from Patriarchy Stockholm Syndrome. Stockholm syndrome is the term used to describe the phenomenon where an abused kidnap victim eventually comes to love and show loyalty to his or her *abusers and kidnappers*.

- You must have a subconscious compulsion for self-destruction.

- You are perpetuating rape culture.

- You are an enabler of rapists, predators, and abusers.

- You must enjoy playing the victim.

And so on.

Please don't misinterpret what I am saying. I do *not* deny that such problems *exist* within the BDSM culture. Of *course* they do. I would simply like to point out that these issues exist in *both* the vanilla world *and* the BDSM lifestyle. This tendency to blame the *BDSM lifestyle* for a whole host of *very real* and serious problems that happen to exist *outside of it* as well is more than just a little *problematic*, in my opinion.

It is wrong to portray the BDSM lifestyle as a misogynistic way of life which *legitimizes* the degradation, humiliation, and torture of women. Yet, it has become not only acceptable, but common, to paint *all* submissives as victims and *all* Dominants as abusers and misogynists with a broad stroke of the brush. Take, for example, this all-too-typical tirade against the lifestyle excerpted from an article entitled, "BDSM is Violence Against Women" on the *Liberation Collective* blog:

> *"We are told that we are not respecting the "agency of women" who choose to engage in BDSM when [we] recognize that playing a submissive role in sexual situations is likely born out of Societal Stockholm*

> *Syndrome. We never, however, blame the women who participate in the practice– our blame sits squarely on the shoulders of men who dominate women. In so blaming, we are told that we are kink shaming the men who like to beat and sexually torture women for fun. A good example of one such man is Snowdrop Explodes who was invited as a "BDSM expert" to talk about BDSM and abuse on the site Womanist Musings. It was revealed that this so-called "expert" had in the past blogged without apology about his plan to rape and murder a woman in his local park."*
>
> *(http://liberationcollective.wordpress.com/2013/01/27/bdsm-is-violence-against-women)*

It is interesting to note that certain phrases from the original excerpt above are nestled in quotation marks. For example, the phrases *"agency of women"* and *"BDSM expert"* are just two of the concepts whose legitimacy is not-so-subtly questioned by the author in this fashion. I can totally understand why the author might want to challenge the very notion that there could ever possibly be such a thing as a "BDSM expert." After all, if one equates BDSM with the hatred and abuse of women, how can anyone be considered an "expert" at it? To most people, that would seem absurd on its face. But why would that same author attempt to delegitimize the phrase *"agency of women"* by putting the same marks around it? Does he or she *truly* believe that women do *not* have free agency to make choices - *right or wrong* - for themselves? Do they believe this *because* she is a woman? If *so*, that would be an odd thing *indeed* for a supposed *feminist* to believe.

The author also seems to have no compunctions or regrets about categorizing *all Dominants* as *potential rapists* through the questionable device of making a single bad apple the *exemplar*. I wish this was an isolated or rare illustration of how the smear campaign against the BDSM lifestyle is conducted, but it *isn't.*

These shrill condemnations of the BDSM lifestyle, as pervasive as they have become in recent years, are about to become a *lot louder*, and *harder to avoid.* For that, we can thank the *Fifty Shades* phenomenon. In an effort to counter some of this anti-BDSM hysteria, many BDSM-related organizations and institutions have come together to produce the following document. It is hoped that law enforcement agencies, prosecutors, abuse counselors, and other professionals will refer to it in cases where there may be doubt regarding whether or not an incident truly represents abuse."

* * * * *

BDSM vs Abuse

(Formulated at LLC III in San Francisco with the assistance of over twenty BDSM organizations.)

The following principles and guidelines are intended to help law enforcement and social services professionals understand the difference between abusive relationships vs. consensual BDSM. BDSM derives from bondage, discipline and consensual sadomasochism and is used to refer to a broad and complex group of behaviors between consenting adults involving the consensual exchange of power, and the giving and receiving of intense erotic sensation and/or mental discipline. Historical usage and dictionary definitions include types of relationships which are not consensual or legitimate.

BDSM includes: "Intimate activities within the scope of informed consent that is freely given."

ABUSE is: "Physical, sexual, or emotional acts inflicted on a person without their informed and freely given consent."

Principles:

The SM-Leather-Fetish communities recognize the phrase "Safe, Sane, Consensual" as the best brief summary of principles guiding BDSM practices:

Safe is being knowledgeable about the techniques and safety concerns involved in what you are doing, and acting in accordance with that knowledge.

Sane is knowing the difference between fantasy and reality.

Consensual is respecting the limits imposed by each participant at all times.

One of the recognized ways to maintain limits is through a "safeword" which ensures that each participant can end his/her participation with a word or gesture.

Guidelines:

Informed consent must be judged by balancing the following criteria for each encounter at the time the acts occurred:

A. Was informed consent expressly denied or withdrawn?

B. Were there factors that negated the informed consent?

C. What is the relationship of the participants?

D. What was the nature of the activity?

E. What was the intent of the accused abuser?

Whether an individual's BDSM role is top/dominant or bottom/submissive, they could be suffering abuse if they answer no to any of the following questions:

1. Are your needs and limits respected?

2. Is your relationship built on honesty, trust, and respect?

3. Are you able to express feelings of guilt or jealousy or unhappiness?

4. Can you function in everyday life?

5. Can you refuse to do illegal activities?

6. Can you insist on safe sex practices?

7. Can you choose to interact freely with others outside of your relationship?

8. Can you leave the situation without fearing that you will be harmed, or fearing the other participant(s) will harm themselves?

9. Can you choose to exercise self-determination with money, employment, and life decisions?

10. Do you feel free to discuss your practices and feelings with anyone you choose?

As good as these principles and guidelines are, I am going to predict with some certainty that they will be absolutely ineffective at stemming the rising tide of anti-BDSM hysteria that will only become more pervasive in the coming years. Logic and analysis rarely prevail against emotion and hysteria. Think modern-day Salem witch trials, only without the trials... or the civility. You may be thinking, something like that could never happen here; not in this country; not like that! After all, we're living in an enlightened age, in a modern society that embraces diversity and tolerance, right?

Right.

Scapegoating

Every decade has its own *boogie men (or women)*. Every affiliation group needs an outsider to be demonized and made into a convenient scapegoat to be blamed for their problems, insecurities, and unspoken desires.

The biblical account of the exodus of the Jews from ancient Egypt tells us how the practice of *scapegoating* began. As part of their ceremonies for the Day of Atonement, the Jews would select a goat from their herd to be led out into the barren desert and left to die. It is perhaps one of the supreme ironies of history that the Jews, *themselves,* later became one of the most horrific examples of scapegoating imaginable when Hitler blamed them for Germany's post-WWI problems and ordered their systematic extermination. The ancient Greeks adopted and then adapted the practice by substituting a *human being* - typically a beggar, cripple, or criminal - to be blamed for all of the community's ills or natural disasters. He would be summarily cast out and banished, often left to die a lingering death in the wilderness from exposure, starvation, or predation.

Eve was made the first scapegoat for Adam's transgression. Pandora was made the scapegoat for releasing evil into the world. Yoko Ono was blamed for the break-up of the Beatles. Mrs. O' Leary's cow was made the scapegoat for the Great Chicago Fire of 1871, which was actually started by O'Leary's careless pipe-smoking neighbor, according an insurance investigation that followed.

Ironically, the term *"scapegoat"* was coined by William Tyndale in his 1530 translation of the bible into English. His dogged determination in making the scriptures more accessible to the common man so enraged the church that he was promptly arrested and put on trial, convicted of heresy, executed by strangulation *and* burned at the stake *post-mortem.* Apparently, when it comes to punishing *heresy*, anything worth doing is worth *overdoing*.

It won't be long before the BDSM lifestyle is made society's scapegoat for the perpetuation of a *rape culture*; for glorifying the systemic hatred, victimization, and abuse of women. Never mind that these societal ills have been with us since the dawn of time. Never mind that both men *and* women are victimized and abused in the general population. Never mind that lifestyle submissives include both men *and* women. *Ignore* the fact that the entire women's movement was built on the notion that women should be able to make their *own* choices and pursue whatever it is that fulfills them or brings them joy.

As long as we're wallowing in cynicism here, let's consider one final bit of irony. Despite the fact that living a BDSM lifestyle carries with it a certain social stigma, recent studies seem to indicate that BDSM may actually be *good for you.*

In 2013, a study by Dr. Andreas Wismeijer, a psychologist at Nyenrode Business University in the Netherlands, demonstrated that people who engage in BDSM lead healthier, happier lives than those in the general population. The BDSM group, as a whole, were on average more extraverted, more open to new experiences, more conscientious, less neurotic, less sensitive to rejection, more secure, and higher in subjective well-being than the comparison group.

Surprise!

Faster Than You Think

Perhaps I'm showing my age now, but I can remember when things were very, very different; and not just BDSM lifestyle things, but *everything*. I *do* realize that I'm probably beginning to sound an awful lot like some *Cranky Grandpa,* shaking his cane at the neighborhood's *young whippersnappers,* telling tales of how he walked twenty miles each way to elementary school in his bare feet through eight-foot snowdrifts, and punctuating each tirade with, *"Get the hell off my lawn!"* I'm guessing that when I finally do get to that stage of my life, I'll probably be waving a bullwhip, riding crop, or pig-slapper. But, *I digress.*

Shit happens, and it happens faster than you think.

Societal change has been coming at us at *light-speed*, with the rate of change accelerating faster and faster in recent decades. Sure, technology is responsible for a lot of that, but it's the rapid resultant transformations in *cultural norms* that should concern us, at least as it pertains to society's perceptions of the BDSM lifestyle. Let's take a quick look at some seemingly *overnight* changes in societal norms.

Remember the pre-Internet age? The advent of the world wide web, *just 25 years ago,* changed *everything*. It is sometimes hard to imagine life before the internet. It was a time when computers were unconnected to the world and big enough to *fill a room*. If you wanted to look up a bit of information, you didn't *Google* it, you went to the local *library*. If you needed a phone number, you searched through an 800 page *phonebook.* Street maps were difficult paper accordions jammed into your car's glove compartment, not on your smart phone or GPS. *Porn* was something you had to visit a *dirty bookstor*e and pay *big bucks* for, instead of saving it off *Tumblr*.

Think on these *very recent developments:* HIV/AIDS. Smoking bans. Same-sex marriage. Civil rights. Birth control pills. Sporks. Sexting. Tasers. Selfies. E-tickets. Wi-fi. We could go *on and on,* but it isn't really necessary, is it? Worldwide societal change *used* to take a lot of time, but that is no longer the case in the twenty-first century.

Today, the pendulum of public perception and acceptance has traveled a wide arc towards acceptance of BDSM born out of curiosity and titillation. Unfortunately, the general public's focus is targeted like a laser beam entirely upon the *bedroom activities* of those in the BDSM lifestyle. The public's general misconception that the BDSM lifestyle is all about kinky sex *actually works in our favor* at this particular point in time, since the advent of the *"sex positivity*" movement.

Once the vanilla world comes to the realization that the BDSM lifestyle does not bear any real resemblance to the fictional works of erotica authors who have never even *dipped their toe* into a BDSM relationship, the pendulum will inevitably swing hard and fast in the *other* direction. Suddenly, the typical vanilla person's reaction will be, "Wait! You mean he *tells her what to do outside of the bedroom?* He *controls* her? He treats her like *property?* Who the *hell* does he think he *is?* This is the twenty-first century! *Nobody* should be able to get away with treating a woman like that! It's *abuse*. It's the worst sort of misogynistic exploitation!"

And so it begins.

This sort of pontification will go *virtually unchallenged*, both in private conversations and in the national media, since there will be few outside of the BDSM lifestyle who know enough about it to effectively refute the diatribe and because it is perfectly *unreasonable* to expect anyone to publicly come to the defense of these alleged abusers of women.

Any efforts by *Dominants* to defend themselves and the lifestyle in general by employing the usual arguments and rebuttals will be perceived as disingenuous and *self-serving* by the public. The harder they try, the worse off they'll be. At the same time, in completely unrelated ways, the stealthy Warrior Princess Submissive is being revered by those around her as being independent, capable, and competitive. She might be that CEO on the cover of Forbes Magazine, the entertainer who blazes her own path to wealth and fame, or perhaps even a candidate for *President of the United States!*

The public will flock to *adore* her for her chutzpah and talent while, *simultaneously*, ridiculing and patronizing those poor, misguided, and brainwashed submissives in the BDSM lifestyle. The public will have *no clue* that the two may, in fact, be *one and the same.*

The Perfect Storm

Make no mistake about it, a perfect storm *is* forming, and it's coming our way. Its sudden onset and fierce intensity will surprise even its most vocal proponents and cheerleaders. Many people who are now in the fetish lifestyle will vainly leap into the fray, foolishly thinking that this will be an orderly battle of opposing ideas that can be fought civilly and rationally. They will quickly learn that they are tragically *wrong* in this assumption, and many of them will pay a terrible price emotionally, socially, *and* financially as a result.

Abuse is wrong, everyone instinctively *knows* this. That is why most people experience an intense knee-jerk emotional reaction to anything that smacks of abuse. Once that emotional trigger is pulled, rationality falls by the wayside.

The problem is, when people are in the throes of that visceral emotional reaction, the entire question of *whether* something constitutes abuse becomes rather *moot*. There'll be no discussion *at all*, no give and take *whatsoever*. Not a peep will be heard about the *validity* of this notion that *BDSM equals abuse*; that the BDSM lifestyle promotes violence against women. *Everyone knows* it to be the *truth*; therefore engaging in any *debate* on the subject makes you an apologist, an *"abuse denier",* and absolutely *complicit* in these heinous crimes being committed against women!

In relatively short order, the phenomenon feeds upon itself and grows in intensity, because *no one* wants to be perceived as *defending the abusers*. The total absence of opposing voices only serves to convince the lynch mob that *everyone must be in agreement,* which emboldens them to push for even tougher sanctions, more draconian laws and penalties, or perhaps even *vigilante justice.* After all, how could anyone *possibly* be in favor of leniency for these abusers of women?

Eventually, BDSM clubs, specialty fetish retailers, and other establishments catering to the kink market will begin to feel a great deal of social and financial pressure to distance themselves from the BDSM lifestyle. One by one, they will quietly divest themselves of the BDSM label, or close their doors after discovering that running a *BDSM*-related business has suddenly become about as socially acceptable as running a *racially segregated, homophobic, or males-only* business. In the end, the die-hard, last-stores-standing will become the intense focus of virulent smear campaigns, picket lines, and boycotts.

Suddenly, simply *being* a member of the BDSM lifestyle will have become about as socially acceptable as being a racist, homophobe, or Nazi.

The Reveal

Let me here and now reemphasize a very important point: I believe the feminist movement is a *good thing*. I support it *wholeheartedly*, without reservation. There are, however, some individuals within the movement, a handful of extremists who are militantly anti-BDSM, who are using this worthwhile cause to pursue their *own agenda* to unfairly attack the BDSM lifestyle and culture. Most people can't or won't see any distinctions or nuances. They view the movement as a homogenous force, speaking with one voice and condemning, *en mass,* BDSM as *abuse*.

This public obliviousness will persist as the voices of the anti-BDSM activists rise in a shrill crescendo until they reach a point of dangerous hysteria that threatens to *criminalize*, in some way, certain activities or relationships in the BDSM lifestyle. When the mere act of being in a D/s relationship or engaging in BDSM activities reaches a societal *tipping poin*t where it is no longer simply socially *unacceptable*, it becomes borderline *criminal*, an amazing thing will begin to happen.

Some Warrior Princess Submissives will drop their stealth cloaks and step out of the shadows to defend the lifestyle and the Dominants that they love. They will *do* this, despite their intense fears and despite a whole host of other very real hardships that will ensue because they are, above all else, *loyal to their Dominants*. They will do it because they are righteous crusaders who aren't afraid to fight the good fight, no matter how unpopular or untenable their positions might seem. They will do it *because they are the only ones who can.*

She will reveal herself as a submissive to a stunned and suddenly perplexed world, announcing for all to hear, *"This* is who and what I am. I am a *submissive.* I am happy and fulfilled in my relationship as a submissive. You loved and respected me *ten minutes ago...* What do you think of me *now?"*

My Two Cents: Final and Next Chapters

Xena: See how calm the surface of the water is?
That was *me* once. And then...
(Xena throws a rock into the water)...
The water ripples and churns. That's what I became.
Gabrielle: But if we sit here long enough it will go
back to being still again. You'll go back to being calm.
Xena: But the stone's still under there.
It's now a part of the lake. It might look as it did
before but it's forever changed.

(Xena the Warrior Princess, Episode 1.03)

One of the saddest things about books is they must all eventually come to a final chapter, and we are now at *this* one's. Conversely, we may also be at a *tipping point* that defines the beginning of the next chapter of the BDSM lifestyle, and perhaps even the next chapter of *your life.*

You needn't necessarily *be* a Warrior Princess Submissive to be profoundly affected by the perfect storm that fast approaches. It could be that she is a friend, colleague, or acquaintance. Perhaps you happen to be someone who *loves* a Warrior Princess Submissive. Or maybe you're simply a member of this lifestyle which will depend upon her for its salvation.

If, on the other hand, you *are* a Warrior Princess Submissive, then you have a *lot* to think about in the days ahead.

We're *depending* on you.

Amarice: I was thinking about what you said, Xena,
about not finding my answers at the end of a sword, and it
seemed to make sense. And then I started thinking about
old Pompey and it seems to me that he found
an answer at the end of yours.
Gabrielle: Amarice, did you not find any
philosophy behind those words?
Amarice: Yeah, kick butt and take names later.

(Xena the Warrior Princess, Episode 4.20)

Appendix A: Glossary

BDSM. Bondage, Discipline, Sadism, Masochism. Some revisionists like to posit that the DS in BDSM can also stand for Domination and Submission, but it is my belief that this confuses the public by blurring the line between BDSM and D/s.

Bottom. A term used in both the BDSM and gay lifestyles to refer to a person in a submissive, passive, receiving or obedient role. The term is usually applied to describe a person's actions and behaviors demonstrated at any given moment in time, rather than his or her deep-seated character and thought-processes. In a nutshell, one's actions may make him a bottom, while one's character may make him a submissive. There is often some overlap and it is entirely possible to be a submissive who is not in the role of a bottom at any given time or circumstance.

Brat. A submissive who is generally well-behaved, but has made misbehavior, teasing, and limited kinds of defiance or disobedience an integral part of her D/s dynamic, preferably with the full awareness and at least the implied approval of her Dominant.

Collar. Collars are viewed by those in the D/s lifestyle in much the same way that rings are considered by those outside of the lifestyle. Just as a ring can symbolize anything from friendship to marriage, or have no symbolism whatsoever, so too can a collar. A collar can be comprised of just about anything, to include a ribbon around the neck, an actual pet collar, custom designed fetish-wear, or even a traditional necklace that only you know the significance of. A collar is simply what the people involved agree that it is, nothing more, nothing less. When a Dominant no longer feels his submissive is worthy of the collar, the submissive may be "released," meaning the collar is revoked.

Consent. Consent, for BDSM purposes, refers to the informed agreement to engage in an activity, scene or relationship, assuming that all parties have a mutual understanding of what is meant by the agreement. Evidence or proof of a partner's prior consent may be difficult to prove after the fact, which can be problematic considering the fact that it is typically the critical factor when it comes to criminal charges such as assault, sodomy, and rape. Even so, documenting consent is a relatively rare thing in the BDSM lifestyle.

Cow/Pig. A submissive is one who enjoys being treated like a domesticated farm animal, and thrives on humiliation, degradation, and abuse from her Dominant and focuses on the real or imagined unattractiveness of the submissive.

Discipline. Traditionally the "D" in BDSM. Generally speaking, it refers to various forms of corporal punishment, such as spanking, caning, beating, flogging, whipping, or slapping. In a more subtle sense, discipline can also refer to the mental discipline required to be a good Dominant or submissive, which sometimes requires a disciplined mindset that allows a person to resist his or her natural impulses.

Domestic. Often referred to as a service submissive. Domestics are expected to perform household duties such as cooking, cleaning, childcare, chauffeuring, and yard work. He or she is typically expected to be sexually available to the Dom, his other submissives, or guests.

Dominant. One who acts in a domineering or authoritative role in life, and especially in relationships. A Dominant may be a "true Dominant" in the sense that this trait is firmly hard-wired into his psyche and he simply doesn't know any other way to be, or he may be acting out a role, whether consciously or unconsciously. A Dominant is defined primarily by his need to control his environment and personal interactions and his skill at being able to do so.

Domme. A female Dominant, sometimes referred to as a Dominatrix or Mistress. Generally speaking, a Domme may refer to any female Dominant, however, outside of the D/s lifestyle, the stereotype typically fits the FemDom Mistress. The correct pronunciation of *Domme* is identical to *Dom*.

D/s. Domination and submission, a phrase which describes a *relationship dynamic* that exists between two or more individuals in a loving relationship. While D/s refers to the dynamic, it defines *who you are in relation to the individual who is your partner.* Who you are at work, or with your children, or around casual friends is *irrelevant* to this paradigm.

Ineffable. A somewhat archaic word, meaning "incapable of being adequately described." It was once a very trendy thing to refer to *God* as being *ineffable*.

Kajira. A female Gorean slave in the tradition of John Norman's series of pulp science fiction novels about the planet Gor.

Kneeling. Kneeling is sometimes used as a euphemism for submitting to a Dominant but is, more often than not, a reference to assuming a submissive posture by sitting on the floor on your knees. Various fetish culture sub-groups may place more or less emphasis on the significance of kneeling. Goreans, for example, teach slaves to assume a series of positions on command from their Masters, many of which are kneeling positions.

Lesser God Dominant. A Dominant *(sometimes referred to as Lord, Prophet, Pharoah, or Pharoanic Lord)* who who thrives on the worship of his submissives. This worship, which can sometimes take the form of highly ritualistic activities and behaviors, exists for the ego gratification of the Lesser God and the practice their own home-grown religion.

Little. A Little is a submissive who finds joy in embracing her inner child. This dynamic often involves behaving, speaking, dressing in a child-like manner, or engaging in typical child-appropriate activities, and may or may not involve sex or other adult-appropriate themes. Also referred to often as *babygirls or lolitas*.

Master. Master is an appellation, title, or even a term of endearment which may be used by a slave or submissive for his or her Dominant. Some Dominants consider Master to be a generic synonym for Dominant, although that practice is generally most prevalent in the Gorean subculture. Other Dominants reserve the use of the title of Master only to those whom they have collared.

Misandry / Misandrist. Hatred or dislike of men as a class; not necessarily targeting men as individuals.

Novice. Someone who has very recently discovered and become excited about the D/s or BDSM lifestyle and has decided that he or she badly wants to be a part of it *at any cost.*

Painslut. An extreme masochist who enjoys or is aroused by sensations of intense and/or prolonged pain.

Pet. A Pet submissive assumes the role of a cherished animal companion to her Dominant, who typically assumes the role of an owner, caretaker, trainer, breeder, or rider. The pet roles *generally* fall into three categories: kittens, puppies, and ponies.

Polyamory. The practice or ability to love more than one person at a time; from the Latin poly (many) and amor (love). Just because polyamory is relatively common in the D/s lifestyle doesn't mean that people in the lifestyle are any better at it than anyone else. It is a profoundly difficult thing to be successfully polyamorous in any relationship, D/s or otherwise.

Polyandry. Refers to a polyamorous relationship in which a woman has more than one male partner. It is typically used to describe a polygamous or plural marriage consisting of a wife with two or more husbands.

Polyfidelous. The practice of being faithful to more than one partner, usually in a polyamorous relationship, is called polyfidelity. For example, a polyamorous Dominant with two submissives may choose to be polyfidelous to his two partners, not engaging in intimate relations with anyone else. This may or may not include BDSM fetish-play, as many people in the BDSM lifestyle do not consider such activity as "intimate." Ultimately, the meaning of polyfidelity must be mutually agreed upon by the individuals in that relationship.

Polygyny. Refers to a polyamorous relationship in which a man has more than one female partner. It is typically used to describe a polygamous or plural marriage consisting of a husband with two or more wives.

Primal. A person who embraces his or her animalistic or primal instincts. Primals are often neither inherently dominant nor submissive by nature. Primals tend to prefer nontraditional poly relationships patterned on the pack or pride dynamic, similar to that of wolves and lions. Primals do treat dominance and submission as a significant part of their interactions with others, but it is something that is fluid and spontaneous, and often established in an ad-hoc, spur of the moment fashion upon meeting someone for the first time.

Pseudo-sub. Someone who may be fairly new to the lifestyle and truly believes that he or she is a submissive, despite overwhelming evidence to the contrary.

Slave. A submissive who cultivates and enjoys the illusion that he or she has no free will. The fact that this is an illusion should surprise no one, since the foundation of any D/s relationship is always consent. Many in the lifestyle consider this a form of consensual non-consent.

Submissive. A person who finds joy and fulfillment in service or submission to another. She is defined by the relationship dynamic that exists between the submissive and her Dominant, *not* by any *other* characteristics or behaviors that she might display elsewhere in her day-to-day life.

Switch. The *classic switch* is someone who is *submissive* to one person (or category of persons) while, at the same time, dominant towards another. A good example is the alpha submissive in a poly Dominant's household, who takes responsibility for the training and supervision of the other submissives in the same house. The contemporary meaning of switch has evolved to refer to a person who can change his or her D/s or BDSM orientation at will.

Top. A Top is someone who situationally or temporarily assumes the dominant, leading, or aggressive role as part of an activity which is usually, but not necessarily limited to, a BDSM scene. A Top may or may not be a Dominant. Conversely and less commonly, a Dominant is not always a Top.

Topping from the Bottom. A submissive's practice of manipulating or influencing the decisions or behavior of a Dominant. This behavior by the submissive can be overt, purposeful, and conscious, or it can be covert, subtle, and unconscious. It is sometimes accomplished with the full knowledge and approval of the Dominant. Other times, the Dominant may be oblivious to it, even if everyone else can see it. The brat sub is the type of submissive that is most commonly associated with this sort of behavior, but in reality, it is practiced by all kinds of submissives, in every category of D/s relationship.

Total Power Exchange (TPE). Total Power Exchange refers to the notion that a D/s relationship or BDSM scene involves not just a surrender of power from one individual to another, but an *exchange* of power. This exchange may involve different kinds of power, and is likely to be asymmetrical, but is an *exchange* nevertheless.

Vanilla. Term used by those in the D/s, BDSM or fetish lifestyles to describe those outside of the lifestyle. It is generally used in the sense that anything that is vanilla flavored (i.e. ice cream) is considered to be unexciting or bland. The term vanilla is rarely used as a serious pejorative or insult, though some people will occasionally choose to interpret it as such.

Verbiage. Okay, what I *meant* was, you wouldn't find the *definition* of the word *verbiage* here. I *do*, however, have a weird compulsion to share the little-known fact that there really *is* an "i" in the word *verbiage*.

Xena: That's the funny thing about people.
Just when you think you've got them figured out
they show a completely different side to their character.

(Xena the Warrior Princess, Episode 3.21)

Appendix B: Silly Shit Mike Makai Says

In my previous work, "Domination & Submission: The BDSM Relationship Handbook," I whimsically began a tradition of including an appendix at the end of the book containing miscellaneous snippets of writing, quotes, musings, and other *Makaisms,* as they've been dubbed by some of my readers. I have - *for better or for worse* - decided to continue the practice in this tome, as well. They are listed here randomly, in no particular order of importance or subject.

In fact, while perusing this part of the book, one would be well advised to remember "Makai's Law," which states, "If it suddenly seems like I am starting to make sense to you, you're *obviously* not paying close enough attention."

# # #

So, I woke up this morning, seriously wondering, "Why aren't they called "*claw*dads?"

We are not defined by what happens to be between our legs, but by how we *feel* about it. Just because I happen to have a penis and testicles between my legs doesn't necessarily mean I must identify as a male. If I *relate* to my significant other(s) as a *female*, then *that* is what defines me as a person. This same principle applies to our D/s orientation. We are not defined by what we *do*, but by how we *feel* about it.

I was discussing BDSM relationships with a Facebook friend one day, when she told me, "I feel as though I am navigating a dangerous mine field, with no map of where everything is buried!"

"Welcome to the club!" I replied, "Sometimes, I marvel at the fact that I still have legs."

My friend laughed and said, "I am not sure I remember filling out and submitting an application for this club!"

"Oh, but it's a *very* exclusive club," said I. "You know the one. It’s that club where people actually *survive and learn* from their mistakes."

Just because you have the freedom to say and do whatever you like, doesn't always mean that you *should*. Master *yourself*, before you would attempt to master (*or* submit to) *another*.

Never, ever doubt that you are worthy of being loved. We are *all* worthy of being loved in some fashion, by someone. The *real* question is, who is worthy of loving you?

Sometimes, I think our lifestyle has become the victim of a *"World of Kinkcraft"* gamer mentality, where people just want to download a cheat sheet or a step-by-step walk-through. Many newcomers yearn to "learn the rules" of the lifestyle as quickly as possible, so they can get right to "winning the game." These are *relationships*, people. Real BDSM relationships, involving real people with real feelings, living really complicated lives. If this was easy, *everyone* would be doing it. Stop looking for shortcuts and easy answers.

Generally speaking, the volume of any proclamation on the BDSM lifestyle will turn out to be directly proportional to its *fatuousness*.

Ladies, *here's* how you get your partner to spank your pussy. First, tell your partner that you like it when he or she *"pets"* your pussy.

Then, while they're at it, you say, "Did I say *pet?* I meant *pat!*" After they *"pat"* it a few times, you just keep saying "Harder... harder!" until... *Voila! Pussy spanking.*

You want *rules?* Here's a rule: I make the rules, and I do it *when* I feel like it, *how* I feel like it. When I *do* get around to it, you're probably not going to like them, so what's your hurry? Chew on *that* for a while.

I usually tell people that I am an *open book.* They sometimes respond by telling me that I am more like an *ebook...* one you can't figure out how to switch on... with instructions written in *Mandarin Chinese.*

I am an incorrigible *word-maker-upperer.* I don't do it to be *obtuse*; I do it out of necessity. The English language is *so flarking limited.* I also thank my lucky stars each and every day for the fact that I have found a way to make a living from being a professional *smart-ass.*

I often refer to people whose current life paths are leading them inexorably to a place they *really* don't want to end up in as *"train-*

wreck-people." Frankly, if train-wreck-people were any good at limiting the damage they did to themselves only, they wouldn't be as problematic as they are. Unfortunately, they invariably insist on having loads of company along for the ride.

Words and phrases have *meaning* in my world. A promise is a promise. A commitment is a commitment. Never again means never again. Last chance means last chance. Maybe means maybe; not yes, not no, not "I'm avoiding your question." You don't get to redefine the meanings of common words to suit your mood or circumstances.

Love shouldn't be about saying, *I love you, therefore you should love me back*, or saying *prove to me how much you care*, or requiring that you shave your back or settle down to have babies. It shouldn't be all about *"what's in it for you."* You either love the person standing in front of you, or you *don't*. Loving the person that you *wish* he or she was is a terrible waste of time and emotional energy.

In my previous book, I proclaimed, "I love redheads. It's not the *color*, it's the *crazy*." Since then, hundreds of *non-natural* redheads have waylaid me to pointedly ask, *"Hey!* What about *us?"* I typically respond, "Anyone who was born blonde or brunette, but is crazy enough to *become* a redhead, is alright in *my* book!" Literally... Now, you *are* in my book.

I'm a little sensitive about my age. Fact is, I just don't like facing the prospect of getting *old*. I knew I had reached the mark that delineates my transition from *middle-aged* to *old fart* when girls stopped telling me, *"Ewww!* You're old enough to be my *father!"* and started telling me, *"Ewww! (insert random disgusted noise here)* You're old enough to be my *grandfather!"* I do take some comfort from Groucho Marx's one-liner, "You're only as old as the woman you feel!" In *that* case, I suppose that would make me 21... and 25... and 32... and 37... and 46...

I'm a typical Aries... Positive, rebellious, impatient, flirty, dominant, charismatic, impulsive, loving, yet sometimes curiously detached. Yes, *detached*. It takes a special kind of person to pull me out of my little shell... *or* my pants.

This is what being a Dominant means to me: Controlling my environment. If you seriously want to be in my environment, then you are agreeing to be a *part* of that. That means sometimes, things are not going to seem very fair to you. I am not sure who told you that life (and relationships) were supposed to always be fair, but it sure as hell wasn't me. Personally, I prefer the word *asymmetrical*. Besides, I never promised you that it would be fair. I only said it would be *worth it*.

I'm patient. *Too* patient, sometimes. When you're a bad girl, I'll be so patient, so calm, so understanding, you just may be tempted to think that it's not such a *big deal*. You would be *wrong*.

Scientia Potentia Est. *Knowledge is power.* There's a reason why most members of the fetish and poly communities don't wear their peculiar lifestyles on their sleeves, and it isn't because they feel that there's anything wrong with what they're doing. It's because it makes them targets for those who are exploitative, mercenary, bigoted, socially inept, or simply mean-spirited.

What of polyamory? Is there a moral standard by which loving more than one person should be considered a sin? Jesus *did* say "Thou shalt love thy neighbor as thyself. There is none other commandment greater." But do you really think Jesus meant to limit his commandment to just one neighbor? Sure, he used the singular form of the word, but... *Seriously?*

When the other fourth-graders were doing science reports on common elements like copper, tin, and mercury, I chose to do mine on Neptunium (a radioactive actinide isotope and the first transuranic element). In sixth grade astronomy class, when the other kids chose to study Venus, Mars and Jupiter, I chose quasi-steller objects. Today, I make my living writing books about the BDSM lifestyle. Obviously, not much has changed over the years.

Real love is *unconditional.* It shouldn't have to be so damned complicated. Whenever you let *coulda, woulda, shoulda, and ought-to-be get* into the act, you're just mucking up something that, if left alone, is truly beautiful in its simplicity and incredible capacity for creating joy in your life and in the lives of others. If I *love* you, I do so *unconditionally.* That's just how I do it; I don't know any other way. If you think you love me, but you're hoping or angling or trying to get something in return, that isn't real love. It's just another form of self-gratification. At best, it's emotional masturbation; at its worst, it is emotional blackmail.

If my life were a zoo, there would probably have to be a sign posted which reads, *"Please do not feed the drama llama."* There really are some very good reasons for this, one of which is the fact that drama llamas tend to have a not-so-funny way of turning their own imaginary problems into very real problems for everyone around them.

A New Life for Amy

I'll finish this section up with a fascinating little story from a recent book signing that I did at a Hasting's Book Store in Wichita Falls, Texas. A woman came into the bookstore and glanced at my table as she walked by, then she stopped and backed up. I said, "Hello, how are you?"

She responded with a distracted *"Hi,"* as she looked at the copies of my book and the colorful flyers on the table. She picked up a book and paged through it a bit, and put it back. She then just *looked* at it in the way a person looks at a $3 chocolate éclair, when she only has fifty cents in her pocket.

I said, "It's really a fun and informative book, I think you would enjoy it."

She smiled and replied, "I think I probably would *too*. My first husband wouldn't like it, but my *second* husband might."

I smiled and said, "Let me guess, you're still with your *first* husband?"

She laughed, "*Yes*, yes I *am!"*

I chuckled as I said, "You gotta love a woman who plans ahead."

She laughed and started to wander away, but then she hesitated and came back to the table, still contemplating the book. I told her, "You *know* you want to buy the book. I'll even sign it for you."

She said, "Oh I *do* want the book, but I am just trying to figure out how to sneak it into my house and keep it hidden from my husband!"

We both laughed, and I said, "Book covers! I bet this place sells book covers!" She remarked that she just needed a bigger purse. Then she mulled aloud the notion of having her daughter *smuggle* the book into the house. I laughed, "Sure, throw your *daughter* under the bus!"

She finally picked up a book and headed to the check-out register, then came back a few minutes later so I could sign her book. I asked, "What's your first name, so I can personalize this for you?"

She thought and thought and thought, and finally came up with a brand new first name for herself: *Amy*.

I realized in that instant what I'd just witnessed. This was her first fifteen minutes in the BDSM lifestyle; the birth of a new identity; the start of a *whole new life* for "Amy."

It was, for me, a profoundly humbling experience to have been a part of that.

Gabrielle: Who *are* you?
Mavican: The name is Mavican.
I'm looking for Xena.
Gabrielle: What do you want with her?
Mavican: I want to kill her. And I understand that
killing *you* is the best way to meet her.

(Xena the Warrior Princess, Episode 5.03)

Appendix C: About the Author

Michael Makai is the author of the Amazon best-seller, Domination & Submission: The BDSM Relationship Handbook. Michael has been a lifestyle Dominant for 37 years, a behind-the-scenes mentor and educator on BDSM and D/s for decades, and has been active in dozens of fetish lifestyle organizations in Europe and the United States. Michael believes that one of the keys to understanding the lifestyle and the people in it is to be able to recognize the very distinct differences between BDSM, which is something you do, and D/s, which is a relationship dynamic.

Michael is a combat veteran and a retired senior Army noncommissioned officer with over 20 years of active military service. He has worked as a marketing consultant, banker, freelance writer, magazine publisher, internet service provider, and a stock market trader. He is an incorrigible word-maker-upperer who enjoys skiing, traveling, playing Scrabble, and raising koi. He currently resides near Wichita Falls, Texas.

www.ingramcontent.com/pod-product-compliance
Lightning Source LLC
Chambersburg PA
CBHW060516290526
45791CB00001B/411
9781497461925